17 Years

in the

Black Room

Written by Susie Sansom-Piper
and Tamara S. Powell, An Excerpt from her life.

AuthorHouse™
1663 Liberty Drive
Bloomington, IN 47403
www.authorhouse.com
Phone: 833-262-8899

Special thanks to Christina Nicole Raetz for her dedicated work to read and edit this book multiple times. Her work was impeccable.

Many Thanks to Narvelle Neves, artist, for the cover drawing rendition.

This book is printed on acid-free paper.

ISBN: 979-8-8230-2652-9 (sc)
ISBN: 979-8-8230-2651-2 (e)

Library of Congress Control Number: 2024910282

Print information available on the last page.

Published by AuthorHouse 06/12/2024

authorHOUSE®

TABLE OF CONTENTS

17 Years
in the Black Room

DEDICATION

To my daughter Barbara (Welton Sr.), my grandchildren Tamara (Marcus), Cynthia (Jerome S.), Welton, and Anthony, my great-granddaughter Brittany, and my two great-greats, Kianna and Brianna – Ma-Ma loves you very much!!!!

Always walk with your head held high. Be great! Do great things, and always serve God. Never quit!

My family that has gone one before me, E.J., Mama and Daddy, Eula (my daughter), and Jerome (my grandson). I love and miss you every single day. You are always in my heart. My second husband, Rev. J.A. Piper, and my many church families and friends, you were all loved.

It is with deep appreciation that I remember the contribution of the late Mrs. Lula H. Moseley, who was among the first teachers in Aycock High, and who so willingly wrote the first history of Aycock for the 1967 reunion activities. Also, the late Miss Alyce Shields, an early Aycock graduate and former teacher in the New York City Public Schools, for her many contributions, including photos and historical facts. I also wish to acknowledge my former Principal, the late Professor O.E.Wilhite, Sr. who for 33 years taught many students, gave timely advice and continuing interest and support in the preservation of the history of Aycock High School.

To all of my many former students and colleagues, thank you for making me the person I am today. Many of you have become great professionals in all walks of life. Many of you have gone before me, and a great number of you are now retired as well. You are my greatest treasure, my pride, and my joy, my legacy! I am grateful to hopefully have deposited something positive in your lives.

Numbers 6:24-26 (NKJV)

"The Lord bless and keep you,

The Lord make his face to shine on you and be gracious unto you,

The Lord lift up his countenance upon you and give you peace!"

PREFACE

I was 5 years old and my brother Jerome, was 3, when our grandmother, Susie Sansom-Piper became our legal guardian. Our mother had been killed in a tragic car accident. Integration of the public schools had just occurred a few years before. As the last Principal to close the segregated school, this memoire begins with a look at the segregated Black Community during her childhood (after 1921) and outlines the challenges she faced both in the integrated school and within the black community. It is a deeply personal look at the treatment of black teachers and students at the beginning of integration and in the years that followed in small town Texas. Hers is a story of resilience, tragedy, and triumph over adversity as she manages to balance the demands of her household, parents, and two small children, while maintaining the decorum and back-bone needed to survive as a Black educator. For 42 years, my grandmother published newspaper articles about the accomplishments of African American students in Rockdale, Tx and sought to educate others about our worth. A lifelong educator, she often presented historical information at schools and churches around Central Texas. She presented before the League of Women's Voters at the Austin premier of Suffragette and at the LBJ library on the 50th anniversary of the Voters Rights Act at the age of 95. She died at the age of 98 in October 2019. Months before her demise, I began working with her to finish this book.

I am a grand-daughter who was caught in the transition years after integration. Shielded on many levels from the racism being faced by our parents and grandparents, I was covertly exposed to systemic racism in the education system and the workplace. I had the great fortune to be raised by my grandmother and great-grandmother, which gave me a unique perspective and foundational determination to succeed. In her last year, I was privy to the internal thoughts written by my grandmother in her youth as she entered the first halls of the white school. Seeing the tear-stained pages written over 50 years ago and listening to her pain as an adult,allowed me to capture the essence and feelings of an African American teacher.

FOREWORD

For the last 22 years, the question has been repeatedly asked of me, "What was it like during the integration years? How did you make it?" The next statement is always, "If *someone* doesn't tell us, we will never know."

Well, I am *"Someone,"* and this is my story.

Seventeen Years in the Black Room is the culmination of my life's work. The tale of my treatment as a Black teacher in the South, bridging the gap between segregation and integration.

It is difficult to describe the many happenings of my time without introducing you to my world before integration. Some things may sound preposterous or unbelievable, but in order for one to grasp the true picture, it must be told "just like it was" during those early integration years. Many of our older people are dying and if our people don't write about them and their experiences, the young people will never know these things.

Please note: It has never been mine to hold grudges or bitterness because of the sufferings of my race in particular. If the truth were known, *all* races have had various sufferings in this chaotic world.

My parents taught me to give love, and love will be returned. Show respect, and you gain respect. So, I say to those whom I encounter each day: may you accept the truth as it is written. My truth. May your hearts be open with understanding, and may you learn valuable nuggets to share forward so that we do not continue to repeat cycles of abuse.

You ask me! So… I'm going to tell you.

This is my personal story. Since my retirement, I have always felt *I* was the designated person to bridge the gap between integration and a segregated world, even from my early beginnings!

Black, brown, white - what is color? It is merely God's way of distinguishing and describing His children. It is the outward cover of a man's body, not the inward personality of His individual self. Color is but a skin texture, a degree or lack of melanin, decorated by curly black hair, long hair, auburn hair, blond hair, or a pair of beautiful brown eyes, black eyes, hazel eyes, or azure blue. Color does not portray the child's inner feeling of love for his teacher, nor the need for the return of that love from the teacher. Black, brown, white - what is color?

During my lifetime, I've met many talented people from all different races and colors. I've taught students who turned out to be physicians, doctors, lawyers, real estate moguls, dentists, nurse administrators, teachers, musicians, star athletes, writers, professors, and great blue and white-collar workers. What I notice most is that it does not matter from what walk of life one originates if one desires to work hard and succeed.

I was the last Principal of the Aycock High School in Rockdale, Texas, a small central Texas town, just before integration. I am proud of my heritage. Proud of the example my parents and grandparents displayed for me, as I am for my children, grandchildren, great-grandchild, great-great-grandchildren, and the many other children I called *mine* over these decades. I am proud of the example I portrayed to many of the thousands of students I have had the pleasure to teach. I tell my story to show people *The Other Side of the Tracks*, provide a window into my thoughts and feelings during the transition from segregation, and show the impacts that came from those years.

I am thankful for the many great people I have met throughout my lifetime, those that transcended color/race lines, and the great friends I have had the pleasure to acquire. Although this book shares some of the painful times, I would be remiss if I didn't mention those citizens that were both kind and color-blind during the transitional days. I acknowledge that those treasured citizens showed me the ropes and stood in my corner. When others had difficulty with integration and not only chose to segregate themselves but showed their hatred, mistrust, and bias daily, there were those that shielded me and helped me in every way they could. For that, I am immensely grateful.

Many of my colleagues are long gone. I am one of the only remaining teachers from the Aycock High School, and today, at 98 years old, my family and friends have dwindled. Many of my students have gone on ahead of me. And they, like some of the teachers I treasured most for their camaraderie and friendship, remain in my heart to this day. Mrs. Laura Petty, Mrs. Artie Williams, and others weathered the storm with me, albeit in different schools. Mr. Lawrence, Mrs. Barlow, Mrs. Pinson, Mrs. Fischer, Mr. Perry, Mr. Alford, and Mrs. Hafer are some of the many teacher friends that I cherish most. They always treated me the same and never attempted to ostracize me, especially because of my color. Some even refer to me as their mentor in some situations.

Some of these colleagues were not part of the transition from segregation at Rockdale Junior High but the aftermath. Nevertheless, these great teachers were part of my story's beginning, middle, and end – one of pride, friendship, fairness, and support. Still, although others were somewhat resentful, they learned to respect the structure and discipline we brought from our community to the integrated schools and sought to learn the measure of respect and control we commanded in the classroom. They may not have liked us truly, but they learned to respect our work.

In the words of St. Francis of Assisi:

Lord, make me an instrument of Your peace.
Where there is hatred, let me sow love;
where there is injury, pardon;
where there is doubt, faith;
where there is despair, hope;
where there is darkness, light;
and where there is sadness, joy.

O Divine Master, grant that I may not so much seek
to be consoled as to console;
to be understood as to understand;
to be loved as to love
For it is in giving that we receive;

it is in pardoning that we are pardoned;
and it is in dying that we are born to eternal life.

My grandchildren never lived in a completely segregated world. That is not to say that there were no injustices shown to them, and in some cases, I did my best to shelter them from the back-handed slights and ill will. It's just that they *rarely* experienced racism in our small town. They went to kindergarten with the same children they graduated high school with. They remained good friends with their fellow students and Rockdale citizens well into adulthood.

Although a select few would utter the racist epithets, they *rarely* reached my grandchildren's ears and certainly did not impact their ability to participate in school functions, activities, or acquire an education. The racial incidents were few and far between for them. For this, I am grateful because I see that the way we paved for our children and grandchildren was made plain and straight. This was a true blessing, considering mere decades before, they would not have been able to walk down the same street as others.

As I look back on that time, I feel saddened that we seem to have taken steps backward in the past few years. People feel encouraged to brazenly use racial slurs and nasty words. Some people attempt to erase advancements made over the past several decades, sowing discord and division wherever possible. Racism has never gone away, but today, people seem free to treat others as inferior, often saying and acting upon whatever they feel. At 98 years of age, I have seen many things, lived through many changes, and I know these are select actions by select groups. Nonetheless, it saddens me to see how far we still have to go.

This book is not meant to offend anyone but simply to share my experience and tell the story like it was. The racial slurs and comments mentioned here are those that were said *to* or *around* me. This book is to tell it like it was for me, my colleagues, my family, my community, and my fellow teachers; to show the feelings beneath the surface of a cool, calm, and disciplined exterior. To show the vulnerabilities and pain that existed as I started into unchartered territory. To share my resolve to survive, determination to overcome, make a difference, and accept the challenges put before me. To show that "I Don't Take No for An Answer!"

Many lives were lost in the transition from segregation to integration. Families were destroyed in the fight for civil rights. Injustices occurred in many states and communities – maybe not as overt in Rockdale, but impactful, nonetheless. Families of educators were separated, much like during slavery, as if it was not important to have a mother, father, and children in the same home or community.

Integration, in simple terms, means to make equal. The word integration was never listed as such in our Constitution, but our great country has always been referred to as the melting pot of nations. To me, school integration has meant the melting pot of personalities. It is the presentation of the facts that:

- People are people regardless of race, creed, or color.
- We all have thinking faculties that are limited to some and gifted to others.
- Talents are not meted out to just one race.
- No race is superior to another.

But, most of all, school integration has meant that **children are children** regardless of surroundings or conditions.

PRELUDE

It seems like yesterday when, in 1954, the Supreme Court, under the leadership of Chief Justice Earl Warren, decided that under the provisions of the 14th amendment, segregation in public schools was unlawful. The major provision of the 14th amendment, ratified in 1868, was to grant citizenship to all persons born or naturalized in the United States, thereby granting citizenship to former slaves and guaranteeing all citizens "equal protection under the law." In order to receive an equal opportunity at receiving a quality education, schools must integrate. For eleven years, the buck was passed, or the edict was ignored - especially by most of the Southern States.

Thus began an era of traumatic history in which many overt decisions were instigated to achieve a reasonable amount of *token* integration, but not without sadness, bloodshed, and the loss of many teaching positions held by Black teachers when schools were absorbed into the "system." At one time, there were eighteen Black teachers, and when we integrated, only four remained. We were retained because we owned homes and property in Rockdale, but others had to find jobs elsewhere.

For the past 55 years, the schools in my small hometown of Rockdale, Texas, have been integrated. Over these years, the tabloids and newspapers were filled with horrible stories of beatings, chasing down by dogs, and even killing of innocent people.

Seventeen of those years, or perhaps I should say nineteen of those years, affected my life greatly, for I was delegated to write and experience the final chapter of a school, Aycock High School, that had existed in this small town for over sixty years. So, in 1967-68, I took my first walk into the integrated Rockdale Junior High and thus began my seventeen years in the "Black Room."

For a seed to reach its greatest expression, it must come completely undone.
Its shell cracks. Its insides come out.
And Everything Changes.
To someone who doesn't understand growth,
It would look like complete destruction.

CHAPTER 1

Community Roots

Life for me began in the small town of Rockdale, Texas.

Before Rockdale became a town or incorporated city, local farmers and store owners recruited Paul Moultrie (later the spelling was changed to Moultry), my grandfather, to move from Georgetown, Texas, to the Rockdale area and serve as the local blacksmith. Blacksmithing in the Moultry family began in South Carolina during slavery. Paul Moultry was born a slave in South Carolina in 1853. Paul learned the trade when he was a very young boy; he and the slave owner's son grew up together in the blacksmith shop. He became a free man at the age of twelve. Shortly after the slaves were freed, he and the slaveholder's son headed for Texas. The slave owner's son stopped in Rosebud, Texas, and Paul traveled on to Georgetown, Texas. This was around the year of 1868. Grandpa Paul established his first blacksmith shop in Georgetown at the age of 15. Paul and his wife, Susie, became parents to 13 children, five boys and eight girls, with one son dying in infancy. His daughters were Sarah, Julia, Mattie Lee, Minnie Ola, Etthie, Frances (Frankie), and Laura. His sons were Edgar(Buddy), Johnnie, Julius (Bose), and James (Jim). All of the children were born at home at 361 Bigger Street, which is now MLK Dr.

Paul was said to have had a good business in Georgetown. According to stories left to his children, he shod the horse of legendary outlaw Sam Bass. In 1882, he made the 50-mile journey to the yet unnamed settlement of Rockdale and became a blacksmith for the Valentine and Hooke's General Store, the only store in the area at this time. He is said to be the first Black in this town. Jack Shields was another blacksmith who came to Rockdale in 1883 from Orville, Alabama. Jack Shield's shop was located in a prairie area between the Missouri Pacific tracks and First Street. Jack Shields was also a procurer for cemetery lots in the original Oakland Cemetery, selling them for a small fee of $2.50 per lot. Jack Shields and his wife Matilda Benson Shields were parents to 17 children. Following these two pioneers to Rockdale were Paul's brothers, Richard, Sambo, and Preston who were farmers.

In 1885, Paul Moultry purchased a shop on a lot where the Gaither Motor Company once stood (now the site of the Rockdale Prison-Main street) and made enough money running it to buy two farms. The first Black business in Rockdale was on the Main Street and later moved to the old Kay Theater lot because of the popularity of horses and buggies, hand plows, and wagons. Blacksmithing was a popular business in Rockdale. Horses were the main mode of transportation, and business was good.

The Moultry family was successful in town. Horseshoes were plentiful, selling for a small fee of $2.50 per lot. Shodding horses netted 25¢ per hoof. All four sons (Julius, James, Edgar, and Johnny) were trained to be blacksmiths. Julius "Bose" Moultry would become my father. James was later called Uncle Jim, and Edgar was called Uncle Buddy. All of them were talented blacksmiths and musicians.

Buddy and Edgar also worked in his shop and later located where the old Kay Theatre is today. Grandpa blacksmithed and operated his shop until his legs would no longer support him and died at the age of 88 in 1936. Grandpa Paul's anvil would later be housed in the Institute of Texan Cultures in San Antonio, Texas.

In 1917, as the World War spread across Europe, the United States War Department realized that the standing army of 126,000 men would not be enough to ensure victory overseas. So, Congress passed a Selective Service Act requiring all male citizens between the ages of 21 and 31 to register for the draft. Within one week of President Wilson's declaration of War, the War Department had to stop accepting Black volunteers because the quotas for African Americans were filled. In all, about 290,527 Blacks were drafted, but due to distrust about arming Blacks and allowing them to fight on the battlefield alongside their White counterparts, they were unable to see combat.

When World War I broke out, there were four all-Black regiments: the 9th and 10th Cavalry and the 24th and 25th Infantry. Only two of these were combat regiments. The remainder of the Black soldiers were designated to labor functions, such as road building or freight handling. My Daddy, Julius, said Black troops were not considered equal during the war. Black soldiers were often treated poorly and exposed to more difficult, hazardous conditions. They also had worse medical care. The food, according to stories told to by my father and Uncle, was atrocious, and their survival depended on eating hard-tack bread or whatever was available.

Two of Paul's sons, Julius and James Moultry, were included in this number. Both were sent to Europe and assigned to the Cavalry. Both had an ability to shod horses. James was assigned to the Cavalry as a blacksmith to keep the horses shod and in a mint condition. Julius was assigned to the Cavalry in Fort Raleigh, Kansas, to shoe horses and later overseas in England and France, serving in the area for nine months and twenty-five days. Julius played trumpet and was also assigned to the US Army Band. When the duties were not required, they were given the task of cooking or digging latrines.

After the war, they returned by boat, landing in New York, the soldiers recalled. They had to remain on the boat for more than a week or until there was a train to return them to Texas. They often had to remain for lengthy periods of time on the boats and trains, with poor conditions. Soldiers were unable to disembark due to extreme Jim Crowism and prejudice in the States after World War I ended. They eventually returned to Rockdale. After the war, Bose established his first blacksmith shop in Thorndale and, in later years, in Rockdale. For more than 50 years, Jim set up blacksmithing in Robertson County in the town of Calvert, Texas.

Following the Civil War, the army had disbanded volunteer-colored regiments and established the regular army regiments of Black troops with White officers. The men in these units were considered heroes in their communities. It was always so interesting to hear Daddy talk about his Army experiences and how they were treated during those times.

As a girl, I always enjoyed the tales he and Mama told about when he began courting Mama after the war. My mother, Eula Bell Crayton Moultry, was the daughter of a mulatto subsistence farmer, one who existed solely on the products of his land, as well as sold to others. My mother was of African American descent, born to two mulattos of Irish, Indian, and Jewish ancestry. She was a housewife, seamstress, midwife, and the first licensed Black nurse in the county. Mama was very fair with long brownish curly hair and blue-gray eyes. She had a long, narrow nose that she called her Jewish nose. She often said her sister, Marzella, could "sit" on her hair.

Mama completed the 9th or 10th grade at the Liberty Hill Community School. All rural children had to attend the *colored* high schools in Rockdale or Cameron to complete their high school education. Mama *wanted* to go to Rockdale; however, farm crops did not do well then, so she was to remain in Liberty Hill. In the meantime, Mama said she met Daddy when they went to Rockdale one Saturday afternoon.

Residents of the two rural communities, Bow Den and Liberty Hill were also considered to be Rockdalians. This is not to be confused with Liberty Hill in Williamson County. Liberty Hill consisted of Bow Den, Tonkawa (across the San Gabriel river), The Hill, and Little Two. Black farmers lived in all of these areas. In the 1800's, my great grandparents, Lizzie Alford Crayton and Mack Crayton, former Tennessee slaves, lived in Bow Den to the west.

Mama said, "Bose use to come to see me in his Hutmobile. Although the visits were unannounced, we always knew when he was on his way to our country home in the Bow Den," which was part of the Liberty Hill Community.

You could hear the sound of the motor eight miles away. Grandpa John would always announce his coming by saying, "Eula, Bose is on his way." Then, at 9 p.m., Grandpa John would announce, "It's 9 p.m., and time for us Jacks to go to bed," which meant it was time for Daddy to leave. Mama wanted to go to Rockdale with Daddy, so, *she* decided that the next best thing was to get married. Mama was only seventeen when they married, and Daddy was 27.

Mama said they had a wedding at home on the front porch. Then, they moved to Thorndale, a small farming town on the south end of Milam County and roomed with Reverend Washington and his wife for a short while. Daddy had set up a blacksmith shop in the downtown area of Thorndale. He sharpened plows, fixed farm equipment, and shod horses. This only lasted for a short while, for the shop was mysteriously burned to the ground. Daddy always believed it was set afire on purpose to give a native Thorndale individual more business. So, they moved to Rockdale, and Daddy began blacksmithing with Grandpa Paul and his brothers Edgar (Buddy) and Johnny. Their shop was located in the spot now occupied by the restored Kay Theatre, used for community happenings. Daddy then opened his own shop on Boga Street. Of the four blacksmith brothers, daddy was the most famous blacksmith.

Mama and Daddy moved to a house on Spruce Street in a section of town known as Speedyville. Speedyville was named for farmer Buddy Speed, who was noted for his peanut crops. Mama and Daddy had hogs and a huge garden and were self-sustaining. Even in the early 1920s, this section of Rockdale was integrated. There were no paved streets, and few owned automobiles. Other citizens weren't as fortunate as my parents, and simply "surviving" became a day-to-day issue. But, throughout their many hardships, people in the community survived by working together.

When Mama and Daddy were first married, she would take in washing for the Phillips, a prominent White family who owned the first funeral home in the area. I can still remember the big, galvanized wash tubs, the rubboard, the old iron wash pot for boiling the clothes, the homemade starch, and the three smoothing irons, which were heated in a little portable furnace with coals, either in the fireplace or on the cook stove. This little furnace and the smoothing irons are still in my possession. They were often used when I went around to speak to students in the 1980s and '90s to illustrate my *Way Back When* series.

Daddy had a first cousin, Almond Moultrie, whom he loved like a brother. He often left Mama in Almond's care whenever he had engagements or had to travel to shoe horses. Cousin Almond was always nearby when he was needed. Mama said, "Almond had carried me to the moving picture show in downtown Rockdale. Bose and the band had gone some place to play for a dance. I was expecting my only child at any time. We barely made it home in the horse and buggy. Almond only left me long enough to go and get Mrs. Annie, the midwife, and then to locate Bose."

At 12:01 a.m., August 23rd, 1921, I made my debut into the Moultry family. They decided immediately to name me after their paternal and maternal parents, thus the name Susie Emma. And *I* narrowly missed being born in a horse-drawn buggy! My mama always repeated this story to my children and grandchildren later in life. I was almost born in a buggy.

Note: I recently found my birth certificate, and the last name should be spelled Moultrie. I never learned why Daddy changed the spelling. I found that the spelling seemed to have changed around the time that Daddy came back or went to France during World War I.

I was a little chubby-cheeked baby with wide eyes and shiny, long, fine ringlets of black curls. Mama said I was breast-fed as an infant. There was no special baby food available to supplement my milk diet. Instead, they mashed to a pulp whatever they ate, and fed me. Mama always said my favorite dish was black-eyed peas, and she never seemed able to fill me up on this dish. According to Mama, I would hold my hands high, and say "more peas Mama, more peas".

Mama made all of my clothes and dressed me like a China doll. Mama said that when I was two or three, in the walking-curiosity stage, I always enjoyed watching Daddy shave with the straight razor. Straight razors were very sharp steel razors that were scraped across a leather strap to get a close, clean shave. So, it was my decision one day to try and shave. Mama said I narrowly missed cutting my throat. The scar has been a forever part of my facial feature on the left side of my chin. It's a constant reminder of my attempt to shave with Daddy's razor.

Those who grew up in the 30's and 40's can vividly recall favorite comic strips such as Magpie and Jiggy, Popeye the Sailor Man, and three munchkins called the Katzenjammer Kids.

The Katzenjammer Kids were created by Rudolph Dirks in 1897, and later drawn by Harold Knerr for 35 years (1914 to 1949). Daddy was an avid reader of the newspaper, and his favorite comic strip was the Katzenjammer Kids. He enjoyed it so much. When we visited Grandma in the Bow Den part of the Liberty Hill community, he encountered his four nephews, Tommy, Bill, Bubba, and Pancho. They were a mischievous lot and always looking to do their own exploration. Because they were always up to some mischief, Daddy called them the Katzenjammer kids. Daddy would say "always up to some trick for the day". Tommy, the oldest, was the boss. Bill and Bubba were the same age, and Pancho was the baby of the bunch. Pancho was the explorer, always delving into some new adventure. Bill was the tinkerer and experimentalist; Tommy was the mechanic and tried to repair and fix everything as a child. We were like brothers and sister.

While I was growing up, Grandma's house was always my favorite place to go. It was about eight miles out in the country, and during the summer, Mama always carried me out to spend a week with Grandma. She taught the girls to piece quilts, make rag and shuck hull dolls, and sew. They were what we call subsistence farmers. That meant that nearly all of the crops or livestock raised were to maintain the farmer and farmer's family. Basically, Grandma and Grandpa grew and/or made everything they used. The men also hunted rabbits, squirrels, raccoons, possums, quails, dove, and other wild game to supplement the family. The farm was a delight to us, for they had cows, horses, mules, chickens, ducks, sheep, hogs, and, of course, an old greyhound to hunt with. I remember most of all the drawing up of water out of the well in the ground. The bucket was attached to a rope and guided by a wheel which could be rolled up and down, and the strange thing was that the water was always cool and very refreshing.

Grandma always had a garden full of all kinds of vegetables. She made hominy by soaking corn in ashes and water until the outside husks were ready to come off. Then she put it in jars for the winter. They even made corn whisky and beer from grains that they grew. They gathered dewberries and mustang grapes and made jelly, grape juice, and wine. They also grew cane to make sorghum molasses.

The most unique thing was watching Grandma catch a chicken from the yard, wring her head off, and douse her in hot water so the feathers would come off easily. There were always three or four grands around, and Grandma would give us salt bacon to go crayfishing in the big tank. We would catch a bucket full of those backward crawling creatures, cut their tails off, peel off the shells, and then Grandma would batter them in cornmeal and fry them for us to eat. They were delicious. Grandma always had homemade tea cakes for us. The cows gave a lot of milk, so we had plenty of milk and cookies to eat.

Grandpa was even a beekeeper, and it was fascinating to see him don his honey-robbing clothes and gather the honey and honeycombs. He never got stung. Of course, we always had to view from a window. Hog-killing time was also fascinating. Most large families butchered two or three hogs or "shoats" per month during the wintry season, this being based on the number of members in the family. Early day families sometimes had 8 to 12 children, for a man's wealth was based on the number of children in his family. To the neighbors, this also meant that they would have food on their tables, for "way back in those days," everyone shared a mess of bones, sausage or ribs.

Usually, in the late fall or early winter, Grandpa would kill a hog. This was an all-day affair. The hog or shoat was then placed in scalding water that had been heated in the old black wash pot. Afterwards, he was placed on boards and very "deftly" scraped to remove all hair. This was done by two or more men, with the neighbors sometimes pitching in to help. Then he would hang him by his hind legs over a scaffold to remove his entrails and other organs. The cutting and carving process began next, plus making and stuffing sausage. Each part of the animal had a particular use, even the "eyeteeth" were saved and used as an assistant to the teething problems of young babies. The women's job was to clean the "chitterlings" and "maw", a soul food delicacy, and the small intestines which were used to stuff the sausages. Cutting up the hog in sections for ribs, backbones, pig feet, hams shoulders, bacon, meaty portions for sausage, and cutting away fats for lard-making were all a part of the day's work. The meat was carefully washed, laid out and salted down with coarse grained salt or factory prepared "special flavored" salt, and then smoked in a designated place for curing and preservation until needed. This process preserved the meat, prevented it from spoilage, and gave it a tasty flavor. Fat was cooked out in the old black wash pot until it reached the oil stage and then it was separated into cracklings for eating and crackling bread, and lard for other cooking purposes. Brains were cooked with scrambled eggs. Pig feet and ham hocks were pickled or boiled and eaten with collard greens and hot water cornbread.

We enjoyed that day, too, for they would let us have the sweetbread to roast over the fire and eat. Sweetbreads are the thymus gland in the throat and the pancreas near the stomach in lambs, calves, and pigs. It all seemed kind of funny, but salting down, smoking, and stringing this meat in the old smokehouse gave the family enough meat to eat all of the winter, and it did not spoil. Looking back over those bygone days, one has to wonder why food didn't spoil and just generally how we all made it.

It was always fun times at Grandma and Grandpa's. On cold days, the families could always look forward to gathering around the fireplace, or the old wood heater to sing hymns, read the Bible by the kerosene lamp, or listen to the battery-operated radio. There was always some adventure or mischief my cousins got into for entertainment. One day, Bill caught a chicken snake. He killed it, removed the entrails, stuffed it with cotton, and laid it in the hallway. It seems that bravery was not in short supply in those days. Becoming a taxidermist was literally unheard of; but my cousin Bill decided he was a taxidermist. Unfortunately, Mama was visiting Grandpa, and saw this creature in the hall. The screams that came forth were piercing, and Bill had to come and prove to Mama that the snake was not alive.

My mother's sister, Aunt Marzella and husband, had a huge farm about 8 miles from town. It was always a great joy to visit them and their 12 children and just to observe the "goings on."

Although they plowed the fields with huge cultivators pulled by mules, most amazing was the large number of milk cows they owned. The morning and evening chores for my age group consisted of milking the cows. And amazingly, they did it by hand! I just watched. I never learned to milk a cow. The milk was always caught in a gallon bucket, then brought in the house ad poured into the numerous crocks on the two six-foot tables. Here they sat until cream formed on the top. This cream was skimmed off and placed in the butter churns with the plunger, and plunged until butter and buttermilk came to life.

My aunt dished the butter out, cleaned it with water and shaped it into pound blocks. The next amazing thing was how she made cottage cheese. The clabbered milk from which she had skimmed the cream, was put into cheese cloth bags and hung in the ceiling until most of the water disappeared. Then we had cottage cheese to eat with the homegrown vegetables, butter to flavor our bread or cook with, and sweet milk, buttermilk, and clabber milk to drink. It's funny how things have changed. In those days, we never heard of any illnesses developing from the way in which we preserved foods.

Life at the farm was great, and as an only child, my cousins were my siblings. We always had a great time together.

Later, when Grandma passed away, Tommy and Bill continued to live with Grandpa. Mama would visit every week to check on them. Pancho and Bubba, Aunt Marzella's sons, lived less than a half mile away so getting together was just a way of life. After Grandpa passed away, Mama took Tommy and Bill in to live with us until they went off to the military. They were like my brothers.

CHAPTER 2

Mama (Eula Bell Crayton Moultry)

Around 2007, as I made notes for this book, I reflected on my Mama. That year, September 17th, she would have celebrated her 105th birthday. As I pondered over this, many thoughts came to mind. Mama was always full of fun. She was crafty and wise. She could always stretch a meal or dollar with her talents. Some experts may have called Mama a frugal individual, for she believed in saving things that others would consider as trash. Yet, she possessed a generous and giving spirit, reaching out to help others in the community and surrounding small towns and country settlements. I suppose that those things were passed on to me.

Mama always did needlework prior to our moving to the flat. She was always well skilled in needlecraft, so she bought a Singer "Treadle" sewing machine. She had always managed to make clothes for me, but then she began sewing for the public. One thing that always amazed me was how Mama could look at a picture, make her a pattern, take your measurements, and then produce a look-a-like garment. She could take mere scraps and make beautiful dresses. Sometimes, patterns were made from old newspapers, and printed flour sacks were sewn and transformed into dresses. Mama fashioned many of the school costumes that were used in various programs. I still have needlework pillowcases, tablecloths, and quilts made by Mama's hands. Later, she managed to purchase an electric Singer sewing machine.

Mama somehow found time to create beautiful things with her hands. One of my favorite crafts that Mama made was the Lightbread Wrapper Hat. It was one of her most unique creations - not one from the store, not a fabulous Milan straw, not a fancy fabric hat, but one made from a collection of light bread wrappers. Particularly the Roman Meal Wheat bread wrappers (plastic bags), as she hardly ate white bread.

The Lightbread Hat is a constant reminder to me of her craftsmanship. The hat had a perfectly shaped crown with a very wide brim, which was wide enough to protect the face from the bright sunlight or other encountered elements. It's not antique! It's not a jewelry heirloom, nor is it a valuable piece of furniture. Its *real* value cannot be priced, for dollars nor cents will ever pay for the immeasurable inspiration and comfort it has brought into my life and the lives of others in my hometown.

Some experts may have called this lady a frugal individual, for she believed in saving things that others would consider as trash. Yet, Mama possessed a generous and giving spirit,reaching out to help others in her community and surrounding small towns and country settlements.

Neighbors could always identify Mama from a distance because of her hat. They would gladly greet her with a friendly hello and perhaps a brief conversation. She donned this hat during the summer months, tending her vegetable garden, watering her favorite flowers, or simply for her daily walk in the neighborhood. When she attended her club and church activities, she wore this hat. If she had to travel a distance to deliver a baby, this hat rode in the car with her. The hat was significant, for it was worn on a head filled with many words of wisdom that she passed on to me and later to my children, grandchildren, and people in our hometown.

Her sayings stuck with me throughout my life:

"Always treat others the way you would like to be treated."

"Respect yourself first of all, and it will be easy for you to respect others."

"Be careful of the company you keep, for it is often stated, if you lay down with dogs, you may end up full of fleas."

"Success does not come easily, but if you work hard enough, you can succeed."

And many others.

Later, Mama developed a new love for the medical field. She completed her high school education through the mail and began studying to become a Licensed Vocational Nurse and Midwife. Mama received her training under Dr. James Lee Dickey, a noted Black physician in Taylor, Texas. She would drive to Taylor (some 30 miles away) once a week to get her training. As a result, she served in a wide capacity in the community for families who could not afford doctor's fees. She delivered more than 300 babies in her lifetime, often without pay. Many times, there was an "I'll pay you later" agreement. Mama not only delivered babies but also treated cuts, burns, measles, mumps, and whooping cough. She treated ingrown toenails and pierced young girls' ears with a needle, thread, and a cork. She was even the favorite dentist of all the tiny tots who refused to let their parents pull their teeth. Instead, the children always made their way to the pink house on the corner for Mama to pull them, simply telling their mothers... "She doesn't hurt."

Healthcare in the community was often taken care of by skilled midwives. Doctors made home visits; however, most people couldn't afford them, so they largely depended on the midwife. Families could not afford the services of a medical doctor, or they either lived too far in the country to request visitation of the local town physician, or perhaps transportation was so limited and uncomfortable, they could not bring the patient into town or maybe the nearest hospital was literally unheard of or miles away. People used the midwife or sometimes improvised and made their own "cure-alls". Many of these remedies and skills were passed from generation to generation and a few are still practiced in many homes today. Few people had vaccinations and there were no immunizations or antibiotics. You were treated with the most logical medication, and hopefully you would get well. Bad colds were sure to be treated with a large dose of castor oil, flavored with orange juice, and an added bit of bicarbonate of soda, to prevent griping, and if the cold was accompanied by a cough, remedies were varied....cow chip tea, flavored with whiskey and sugar, horehound candy soaked in whiskey to make a cough syrup, honey mixed with vinegar; hog hoof tea made by boiling the hooves of the hog that had been salvaged during hog killing time. The patient was often "greased down" from head to foot with warmed tallow (cooked sheep fat) mixed with turpentine, or some other vile smelling salves. Or a flannel poultice containing a mixture of snuff and tallow was placed and worn on the chest. A salve was also made from boiled hog testicles, and also used to treat chest colds. Chills and fever required a variety of treatments. Sometimes the patient was bathed down in extremely cold water. If both chills and fever persisted, the patient was wrapped or packed snugly under heavy piles of cover to "sweat it out", or an alternate method was to count the number of chills, get a piece of cord string, and tie the number of chills in the string, soak each knot in turpentine, and tie the string around the patient's waist. Quinine was one of the few "bought" medications used for fevered conditions. Chamomile weed (earth-apple) tea was also a favorite remedy for this condition. Whooping cough, often an epidemic among children, was treated with cut-up onions soaked in sugar, and the remaining juice was fed to the patient. Measles, another sure epidemic, was "brought out" with boiled "dried-out" corn shuck tea, which was fed to the patient for 3 or 4 days. For sprained ankles, wrists, etc., clay poultices made of red clay and vinegar were packed on the sprain. Mullein leaves gathered from the woods and boiled was used to treat swellings. Tobacco juice or snuff solutions was spread on a wasp or bee sting. Mustard plasters made from the mustard plant were used for backaches, or a leather band or copper wire bracelet was worn, around the wrist to treat arthritis. Vanilla flavor and tobacco was used for the toothache; to avoid infections from nail punctures, the foot was soaked in coal oil. Rheumatism was often treated with a rubbing liquid made from vinegar, salt, and crushed cedar leaves. Garlic was used to treat high blood pressure. Internal soreness was treated with turpentine and sugar or coal oil and sugar.

Babies also had their share of home remedies. A small bag of asafetida was made into a necklace and tied around the neck for immunization purposes. Colic was treated with a teaspoon of breast milk that had been flavored with several puffs of smoke from a cigarette blown into it; a teething baby wore necklaces of a hog's eye tooth, or three wood lice or a group of red ants sewed into a bag, and sometime a silver dime made into a necklace was worn. Impetigo sores were treated with sulphur and yellow vaseline and frequent baths in warm Epsom Salt water. Come spring, families would take to the woods to gather Poke salad, for this was considered a way to rid the system of impurities. The prickly pear was also picked in its soft stage, with thorns removed, diced, boiled, and eaten alone or with scrambled eggs. Another form or cactus was sometimes beaten to a pulp and applied to treat cuts and bruises.

When people died, there were no black morticians initially. Blacks buried their own. The body was placed on a "cooling board", with a saucer of salt on the deceased's stomach to prevent swelling. Neighbors, friends, and family members built the pine box coffin that was often lined with cheesecloth to protect the body.

Later, Mama began working for Dr. J.T. Richards, a White physician, when he opened a clinic in Rockdale. She worked for Dr. Richards until her retirement but remained busy afterward. Mama was fiercely independent and didn't mind expressing her imminent thoughts. She proved to be a friend to all people regardless of race, creed, or color. She sewed garments, nursed people back to health, and delivered babies for all races during the '40s until her retirement as the first Black nurse in Rockdale, Texas. The Texas Legislature gave her accolades for her contribution to nursing and Milam County. Mama served as a nurse and midwife through the next twenty or more years.

After her retirement, Mama became a pedicurist for the elderly and well-to-do people. She often carried her little kit to the nursing home and cut people's toenails. I still remember the day she brought home a box of toenails to show. The nails had grown so long and thick that they curled into a half-moon and were well over an inch long.

I can still remember Mama's encounter with a UFO in the '50s. She had been to Thrall, Texas, to deliver a baby. She said frightfully, "This thing hovered over my car for the next twelve miles. I never told anyone because they probably wouldn't believe it."

She always took time out for recreation and had four special pals that she traveled with. Although they were always together, Mama always tried to insert a bit of fun and, at the same time, wanted to have a cultural atmosphere. Miss Beulah could frequently be found holding down the passenger seat in Mama's little green Pinto. Their favorite place was Andy's Café, just down Highway 77 outside of Rockdale. Andy's was known for their fresh fried catfish, and Mama's favorite cold schooner of Schlitz's malt liquor beer. Mama and Miss Beulah would go to Andy's on any given day for the fish or a delicious hamburger. It was always funny because Mama called Miss Beulah to ride shotgun, but she always returned complaining about her table etiquette with a bit of laughter, saying, "I enjoy Beulah, but she gets on my nerves. She always has to cut her hamburger with a fork. Who ever heard of such?"

Her next traveling companion was Ms. Alyce Shields, who was highly educated and knowledgeable, but again, Mama was disdainful of her habit of cutting her hamburger into quarters. She would say, "Alyce cuts her hamburger into four parts, eats one part, wraps the other up, and sticks it in her purse for later meals." This was so embarrassing during the '50s and '60s.

Every Friday found Mama traveling to Cameron to pick up Ms. Fannie so that they could travel to the fish place in Buckholts. We always cautioned her about driving on the highway at her age, for she drove at such a slow pace. She reminded us with a little chuckle, "I know what I am doing. I only drive on the access roads." Can you imagine them driving 25 miles per hour on an access road of a main highway?

Mama's fourth buddy, Miss Jennie Shields, lived to be 107 years old. She was the pride of my hometown, for as a centurion, she rode in airplanes, on the fire truck during parades, and on a motorcycle. Her thinking ability was superb. I called her Mama's party pal. Mama often baked her cakes, and together, they would enjoy their wine sipping and cake eating. There happened to be a time when they were celebrated a little too much, and my 87-year-old mother couldn't drive home (down the hill). According to my granddaughter, Mama called her to walk up the hill and chauffer her home, cautioning her not to tell me what had happened. Finally, my grandson spilled the beans, and Mama turned on the waterworks when I gently chided her, dramatically crying, "Y'all don't want Mama to have no fun," sniff-sniff, sob, sob.

My Mama and her pals intrinsically enriched my life. They taught me that:

- You are never too old to enjoy good friends.
- You are never too old to enjoy life in general.
- Most of all, you are never too old to drive if you have mental alertness and activity of limbs.

CHAPTER 3

Daddy: Julius "Bose" Moultry

The Village Blacksmith
Henry Wadsworth Longfellow - 1807-1882

Under a spreading chestnut-tree
    The village smithy stands;
The smith, a mighty man is he,
    With large and sinewy hands,
And the muscles of his brawny arms
    Are strong as iron bands.

His hair is crisp, and black, and long;
    His face is like the tan;
His brow is wet with honest sweat,
    He earns whate'er he can,
And looks the whole world in the face,
    For he owes not any man.

Week in, week out, from morn till night,
    You can hear his bellows blow;
You can hear him swing his heavy sledge,
    With measured beat and slow,
Like a sexton ringing the village bell,
    When the evening sun is low.

And children coming home from school
    Look in at the open door;
They love to see the flaming forge,
    And hear the bellows roar,
And catch the burning sparks that fly
    Like chaff from a threshing-floor.

He goes on Sunday to the church,
    And sits among his boys;

He hears the parson pray and preach,
 He hears his daughter's voice
Singing in the village choir,
 And it makes his heart rejoice.

It sounds to him like her mother's voice
 Singing in Paradise!
He needs must think of her once more,
 How in the grave she lies;
And with his hard, rough hand he wipes
 A tear out of his eyes.

Toiling,—rejoicing,—sorrowing,
 Onward through life he goes;
Each morning sees some task begin,
 Each evening sees it close;
Something attempted, something done,
 Has earned a night's repose.

Thanks, thanks to thee, my worthy friend,
 For the lesson thou hast taught!
Thus at the flaming forge of life
 Our fortunes must be wrought;
Thus on its sounding anvil shaped
 Each burning deed and thought.

Julius Moultry was the fifth son in a family of thirteen, born to Paul Moultry and Susie Nunn Moultry in Rockdale, Texas; Daddy was the seventh child. His name was Julius, but everyone called him Bose. Grandpa Paul trained his four sons to become blacksmiths, and my father was the third blacksmith in the family. In the early days, boys had limited education, so Daddy was only able to complete a 5th grade education, and by the age of 12, he was a full-time blacksmith in Grandpa's shop. Yet, this limited education enabled him to read, write, and have enough mathematical skills to operate his own business. Notably, all three Moultry brothers, except Uncle Jim, worked in the same shop during the early years.

On July 9, 1919, Daddy returned home from World War I to resume his horseshoeing. It was on that day that he met Mama. According to Daddy, he was planning to head to Oklahoma to set up shop; but, he couldn't leave after he saw Mama. Daddy started working for B. Ashby in a shop situated on a lot across the street from the present Post Office. Daddy was famous for his horseshoeing ability and soon earned the title of being the best "horse-shoe-er" in the southwest. Because of this, he was often recruited by owners of racehorses to shoe horses at the racetracks in Fredericksburg, Texas, and the states of New Mexico and Arizona. He had been paid as high as $85.00 to shoe one racehorse at a time when the going rate in his shop at Rockdale was $1.50. Daddy recalled in a 1959 interview that his customers believed he could take a hammer and an anvil and make a watch.

White folks needed Daddy, my grandpa, and the brothers (Uncle Jim, Uncle Buddy, and Uncle Johnny) to build their carriages, shod horses, make iron tools, and sharpen plows. Unfortunately, two brothers died ill health and untimely deaths. Uncle Johnny was an alcoholic, and one day, he set himself and his house on fire. Then, Uncle Buddy died, leaving Daddy as the only blacksmith in town. My Daddy was a quiet but stern man. He was well respected as the only blacksmith left in that area. Farmers and townsfolks needed him to keep working. I remember Daddy telling *anyone* that came if they didn't like his work to "get the hell out of his shop." He never had any trouble with them after that.

Daddy designed and created from scratch many of the branding irons used by cattlemen and made gate emblems for the ranches. Daddy formed many emblems for large ranchers from scrap iron, such as the Coffield Domain. He made barbeque pits from iron drums. He learned welding as self-defense after the automobile startup sent blacksmithing on its inevitable decline. He was also famous for building horse trailers, taking the chassis from automobiles, and then constructing a trailer from the ground up. The downside was that, as a self-made businessman, he never patented many of his ideas and his talents with the forge. Through the years, I have often lamented that we knew nothing about patents in those days.

When he went into business for himself, he opened the shop on the lot formerly located on Main Street. His first blacksmith shop in Thorndale, Texas, was mysteriously destroyed by fire in 1924. Daddy always believed it was set afire on purpose to give a native Thorndale individual more business. From this location, he moved to Rockdale, Texas, to a lot located directly behind the present-day Citizens National Bank on Boga Street. His last location in 1924 was just beyond the Missouri Pacific Tracks, about one block west of South Main Street near the Main-Mill corner. Although Daddy was an independent businessman, he was often paid with a supply of vegetables, cured meat, or some other product. During dormant seasons, he and his buddies always enjoyed domino games on their homemade table in the back of the shop.

Daddy also purchased a trumpet for $25 and taught himself to play. He said that his 10-piece brass band was the first music heard at the local Juneteenth celebration. During the early days, celebrations were held in the form of church picnics; most of the families prepared their own food, which included barbecue, baked sweet potatoes, salad, roasted corn, pies, cakes, sodas, and they would all gather on the church grounds under canopies and spread the food on oil cloth on the ground to be eaten by all. As time progressed, the local Fair Park became available. Daddy and his brothers used to sponsor the local Juneteenth festivals at the Rockdale Fair Park. People from many surrounding towns would come to share in the Pride of their Freedom. There was always a parade, special speaker, and singers from the local churches. A dance for all, with a local orchestra or prominent fiddlers furnished the music. Baseball games were also a special event. Other amusements consisted of barefoot races, drop the "hankie", tit-tac-toe, crack the whip, blind man's bluff, wrapping the May pole, Little Sally Walker, hide and seek, jump rope, greasy pig, hop scotch, farmer in the dell, London bridge and many others. These were mostly games played by the smaller children. The young men and young ladies had gig rides (a two wheel gig drawn by one horse), barefoot races, serenading, boxing, and horse and buggy races. Some families celebrated at their homes with relatives gathering to help in the celebration.

I can still picture him as he walked to his blacksmith shop each day. Daddy had a reddish-brown complexion, a wide nose (that I inherited), and fine, straight hair. He had strong powerful arms that he said had been good to him and his family. He could often be found with overalls and a cigar hanging from the side of his mouth. His old felt hat wore signs of coal dust from the fuel used in the hearth where he heated and tempered the iron to sharpen farming tools or perhaps made a special emblem for the big ranchers to brand their cattle. His faded blue overalls had many patches over the holes that were burned or simply worn through. August 8, 1966, Daddy was featured in an article by Leon Hale called *The Making of A Good Blacksmith. My father said, "The only job I ever had in my life was blacksmithing. A colored boy always used to go to the cotton patch to make him a little 19th (June) money. I went one time when I was about 14. I went out to chop cotton for old man Ben Reed. And he told us, 'Now, boys, 'no use in killing yourself. All you got to do is keep up with that little girl, yonder.' Well, the girl was about my age, but I never got close enough to her to see what she looked like. Nor did I say a word to her. I got so far behind; others had to come and help me out twice before we got to the end of the first row. And they helped me out again to finish up the second one. And when I got through it that first round, I hung my hoe on the fence, walked back to town, and I had not been in a cotton patch since."*

Julius Moultry slapped at a fly on the leg of his blue overalls as he sat in an open door of his shop in Rockdale, where he had been a blacksmith ever since he walked away from that cotton patch 58 years ago. He wore a felt hat and house shoes, and in his big right fist, he waved a plastic fly swatter with netting that was almost worn away. In his left hand was an old pipe with the dead cigar butt stuck in the bowl. But now he says, sitting there at the door to his shop, "I can't do no more work. Got high blood pressure. Oh, and once in a while, I get up and do a little something. But I ain't particular about it."

The sound of the Smith working came from the back of the shop. "I got me a boy back there. J.D. "Zero" Miller been with me about eight years. I taught him everything he knows. And he can do anything. He'll shod five or six horses here a day. That horse piece shodding now belongs to the High Sheriff from Cameron. I'll tell you how blacksmithing has changed. Back in the day, I paid $5.75 for a keg of horseshoes down the same keg cost me $38.00. I used to pay a good Smith $1.50 to work a ten-hour day, and now I pay him $10.00. I used to charge $1.50 to shoe a horse. And now I have to charge $6.00."

"Sometimes the making of a blacksmith, it's a birthmark. My Daddy was a Smith and taught me all I knew. Me and my three brothers all made blacksmith. My Daddy never whipped a one of us awake in his life, but he had a way that made you rather have a licking. I'd shoe a horse, and he'd look at it, and he'd say, 'Now you rasp over there one of them nails off and pull them out. And you shoe that horse the way I tell you, not the way you want to do it.' And I learned, and I'll say, I never saw a man Black or White that could beat me shoeing a horse. Except my daddy, about 90% of my businesses from the White people. I want to say, this Rockdale's got some of the best White people in the world. And I'll show you what I mean. While that Henry Smith passed, an old colored fella here in this town and the richest man in the County, Mr. H.H. Coffee, was sitting in that church for the funeral. And he went to the graveyard after that, too." Moultry later told Hale about his first airplane ride, but that would have to wait for another day.

In 1968, Daddy received a letter from the Institute of Texas Cultures Hemisphere Headquarters in San Antonio, requesting information on the art of blacksmithing dating back to his father's entry into Texas. An anvil picture and résumé of his blacksmithing are now part of the Ethnic Culture Program at the Institute of Texas Cultures. He was also requested by the Institute to make a branding iron for the Festival of the Smithsonian Institute in 1970 to represent Texas Cultures in Washington, DC, along with an invitation to attend an all-expense paid trip given at the same time. Unfortunately, a substitute replacement had to be made because of his ill health. Daddy continued the family trade there in Rockdale until his ill health. Daddy was Rockdale's blacksmiths for over 62 years. He passed on his many skills to his protégé, J.D. "Zero" Miller, keeping the blacksmith shop open to span the entire history of blacksmithing in Rockdale.

In 1978, at the age of 84, Daddy passed away in Rockdale, Texas. An era of Rockdale history quietly ended. J.D. "Zero" Miller continued to operate the blacksmith shop after Daddy's death for 19 years, finally closing the business in 1997. By this time, blacksmithing had pretty much been replaced by newer technology, and the shop was often used for auto repairs. Welding became Zero's main business. He also worked on cars. There's just no call for blacksmithing anymore. Today, the blacksmith shop of Julius "Bose" Moultry no longer stands. The old building, scarcely noticeable at the back of the Rockdale Building Material Center, was sold to the busy lumber yard. Today, a miniature blacksmith shop and replicas of some of the tools he used are behind the museum in town. A park near where the old Aycock stands is named after him and my grandpa, Paul Moultry.

These are a few of my memories of Daddy, but my fondest memory is a piece of advice that he gave me at the beginning of my teaching career. I was experiencing some unfavorable conditions. He always called me "Bug". Daddy said "Bug, when people mistreat you, beware. Always treat them very nice but feed them with a long-handled spoon."

In my heart, I can always say. "Thanks, Dad". He was a man of few words, but he was my confidant.

CHAPTER 4

A Segregated, Integrated Background

Rockdale was a proud town of unselfish living. It was an average small town and possessed the typical small-town layout. In Rockdale, the movement for civil rights was not as violent and disruptive as in other parts of Texas. Blacks, Whites, and Hispanics have always managed to peacefully co-exist in our town, for slavery and the mindset that came with it was never fully known or explicitly expressed to be an integral part of Milam County. The "cut-off lines" for slavery and plantations were said to have been in the Robertson County area. This is not to say that there were no people who were prejudiced, but that it was not widely expressed.

Our town had always been segregated yet integrated, for in each designated section of town lived people of all races. Early Rockdale was centered on the railroads. Rockdale had two main streets, Main and Cameron. By the late twenties, only a few people had or could afford automobiles. Transportation was limited to buggies or wagons. The city limits were near what is called today, Rainbow Courts on the east, the old Lowenstein house to the west (now a law office on Bowser), near the Coffield pipeyard to the north, and the Roberts FM 908 intersection, to the south.

The majority of Blacks lived across the tracks on the east side of town and Whites on the other side of town. My neighborhood consisted of Blacks, Hispanics, and poor Whites. My neighbors and I played together as children. Across the tracks lived other Blacks who had to travel across the tracks to go to the Black school. Although our neighborhoods were not particularly segregated, the schools were separate. The only section of town where integration may not have occurred was the so-called "College Hill," where the storekeepers, lawyers, and aristocrats lived.

My friend Lulu lived next door. She and her family were Mexican. We played in the graveyard between the school, farm-to-market road, or yard. We made mud pies and set them in the sun to "bake," gathered China berries and pretended that they were our peas, gathered and ate a weed called sour dot grass, and used wildflowers for decoration. Lulu and I played with homemade dolls. We cut paper dolls out of catalogues, as well as their clothes. We also went to a large barn in the Davis family's yard. Other children, Mozell, Eural, and I enjoyed climbing in the loft and playing together. There was always a sense of fair play and enjoyment. We could play without referees or special supervision, whether on the farm or with friends in town. We gathered on sand lots to play a game of softball. We created our own diamond with bases made of rags filled with sand. In later years, adults would line it off with white lime. Sometimes, we had a real bat and ball, and other times, we only had a wooden plank for a bat. Nevertheless, we happily played the entire game simply for the fun of it.

Little girls often played jacks or jack stones as they are sometimes called. We always managed to have a small rubber ball, but many times, we had no jacks. So, we would gather 10 tiny stones about the size of a jack and played our game beginning with ones to ten.

We also learned how to shoot marbles with the little boys. Other childhood games included Wolf Over The River, which was a game of pull and tug; Ring Around the Rosey; Hide and Seek; Pop the Whip, and Jump Rope, which is still popular today.

Small tanks or ponds were always nearby, and they were usually filled with crawfish. Mama taught us how to bait a string to catch them. We used a tiny piece of salt bacon tied at the end of the string. When they used their claws to take hold, we pulled them out of the water and placed them in a tin pail. We would cut the heads away, peel the shell from their tails to secure the meat, and then Mama would fry them in cornmeal. What a delicacy! Lulu and I played together until I was six years old, then her family moved away to Thorndale. My neighbor Ms. Eva took in sewing, and I enjoyed watching her sew on her Singer Treadle sewing machine. We also enjoyed exploring the fields and searching for sour grass which we ate with salt, and butter nuts which grew under the roots of some flowering plants. To this day, I have never seen these items anymore. I often wonder if they became extinct or were inevitably destroyed by city growth. Lulu and I played together until I was six years old, then her family moved away to Thorndale.

I also had a beautiful shaggy dog named Fly. Mama would allow me to venture out of doors, for she knew that Fly would be my bodyguard. A barbed wire fence surrounded our yard with a wooden homemade gate at the entrance. Fly would never allow anyone to come through the gate unless she was given the right command. Many memories are cherished from my pre-school years. My parents worked hard to survive.

In attempts to provide for their families, many people became tenant farmers (they paid to live on the land owned by the farmer and worked their own crops), and others turned to sharecropping (where they lived on the owners' land and received a share of the profits of the crop). Others simply hired themselves out to plant, chop, pick, or gather the crops, following the seasons harvesting routes from East to West. My parents always kept a big garden. Mama canned vegetables and made homemade preserves, jams, and jellies. They also kept chickens for meat and eggs. Milk was purchased from Mr. Warren on Third Street or Ms. Shine on Cameron Avenue.

People also supplemented their pantry with the bounty of natural resources in the Rockdale area. They fished and hunted doves, rabbits, squirrels, raccoons, and armadillos, grew gardens, picked mustang grapes and dewberries, or used seasonal fruits to make wine and jelly. Hogs and cows were allowed in town; hog killing usually rolled around during the second month of winter. Gardens products and meat from "hog-killing" time were shared with neighbors. Meat was cured and stored on the back porch in boxes with salt and made into sausages or stored for the lean months ahead. However, I do remember a time when someone stole all of our winter meat. No one ever discovered who the culprit was, so it was just a loss. But God always provided a way for us to survive. Mama had canned a lot of fruits, and jellies, and vegetables. Aside from these one-off incidents, people in the community worked together. Neighbors traded and shared work and goods to make ends meet.

It seems as though the winters during the Depression years were much colder than today. Could it be that we were so dependent upon that one fireplace or that little tin heater? We had a big pot-bellied stove. One had to constantly chucked wood, corn cobs, or any other burnable thing into them to try to stay warm. I can remember Daddy raking ashes over the live coals so that fires could easily be started the next day. Usually, the heating elements were located in the kitchen and one specifically designated room. The bedrooms were not heated, so you had to climb into bed and get on the cold sheets, then pile all of the homemade covers on your body. No bed in the bags for comfort. We had specially crafted quilts. There was a coal shed outside and next to it was the outhouse. The girls' outhouse was on the north-side and the boys' out-house was on the south-side. Outhouses in the earlier days were cleaned monthly by a scavenger man with his barrels on a wagon pulled by mules.

In those early days, everything that wasn't wearable was sewn, and especially the worn-out overalls or wool garments. My mother and grandmother deftly created what was called a britches quilt. Once you were covered with this, you could hardly move. And when the britches quilt wore out, it was covered with an attractive piece of calico fabric to create a beautiful comforter. Nothing was destroyed or passed on to charitable organizations. It was a matter of survival and survive - we did just that.

In spite of stark conditions, there was an abundance of love and cooperation in the community. While sometimes, there were conflicts within the race between those that were fair skin vs. dark skin, with different hair textures, or dialect, the overall spirit was one of cooperation and comradery. Unfortunately, this has been an ongoing challenge in the black community since the days of slavery. The complexities of which are too deep to expound upon in this book; but, an underlying challenge, nonetheless.

Neighbors looked out for each other and their children, regardless of sometimes petty differences. There were no streetlights across the tracks. Roads consisted of only gravel or mud. There was no indoor running water. A few people had wells from which they used wooden buckets or pails to draw up water. Others had cisterns or barrels to catch rainwater. Some hauled up water from the city pump which was located near the old cemetery. Water was 25 cents a barrel. In addition, there were only outhouses to relieve oneself.

People often lived in three-room houses that were sometimes filled to capacity with six or seven children. During those days, there was a lot of trust between neighbors. Doors were not locked, even when you had to leave home for a short while. During the hot summer months, a quilt spread out on the front porch, or an old iron cot in the backyard was often used as a respite for a good night's sleep.

When you had a nickel in the '30s and early '40s, you felt that you had struck gold. Just think, five huge pieces of bubble gum that you could toy with, a double dip ice cream cone, a bag of popcorn at the movies, a hard candy bar, and an all-day sucker! Yum Yum! A glass of red water at the fairgrounds on Juneteenth days, and you and your buddy could pool those nickels together and bug a big fish sandwich to share. The least things in life brought pleasure during these times, leading to total tranquility and a sense of appreciation.

Two train tracks for passenger and freight trains ran daily through Rockdale. They were the San Antonio & Aransas Pass, and the Missouri Pacific. Their lines intersected east of the Coffield buildings on Milam Street.The SA&AP ran north and south between Waco and Yoakum. Its little two-car passenger train, named the Dinky by Rockdale residents, ran twice a day. Children who lived on Spruce and Boga streets looked forward to watching this train daily. The Union Pacific railroad through Rockdale was once the Missouri Pacific and before that, the International & Great Northern (I&GN). Early African Americans in Rockdale lived north, south, east, and west of the two rail lines. Lyle Tindle and his sons J.B. and M.C. Tindle were some of the early railroad workers. Once I married and started a family, Mr. J.B. lived next door to us for many years. The frequency of the trains through town brought beggars hopping from town to town. Even then, "homeless people" existed but were called "hobos" at the time. They brought no fear or unpleasant thoughts, for everyone understood that they were simply people trying to survive day by day. They would come to your back door and ask for food. While they stood patiently at the door, the lady of the house would prepare a sack lunch consisting of homemade biscuits, sausage, teacakes, etc. They accepted with a courteous "Thank You" and left, walking towards the railroad tracks to "hop" the next freight train in search of a better life. While sometimes there was fear when venturing out from the community, there was also a lot of happiness within. Citizens helped each other. Children worked and played together without fear. Though poor in wealth, there was richness in determination and spirit. There was community love and cooperation. Although segregation existed during these early years, few major encounters were heard of in my town.

Criminal acts were virtually unheard of... perhaps a fistfight or a bout of drunkenness, but civility and "getting along" were features that gave this small town a special uniqueness. Occasionally, someone may have been arrested for an overnight stay in the segregated calaboose, but crimes that involved trials or longtime incarcerations were virtually unheard of.

But for every general statement, there is always at least one exception. One such incident is when a 17-year-old student was "accused" of being a "Peeping Tom" on the White side of the tracks, and he was "escorted" out of town. This happened in the late '30s. He left his home and never returned until almost 30 years later, in 1966. He said, "I was innocent of this crime, but if I had stayed around, I don't know what the results would have been."

Segregation was not only in our schools and community but was exemplified in eating facilities. Downtown, the cafes were segregated. Blacks ate in the back and Whites in front. At the diners, Blacks could eat in the kitchen of the café at a small, designated corner table. Or, if food was purchased at Dairy Queen, individuals would have to leave on foot or via automobile, if available, and retreat to a comfortable place on the side of the road to eat. Segregation was exemplified, as I have described, in the restrooms, restaurants, living locations, water fountains, train stations, and parks by designated signs; "Colored Men Only," "White Men Only," "Colored Women Only," "White Women Only!"

Two stores in my town were operated by Whites: McVoy's and City Food Market. The two grocery stores in the middle of the road had just about everything one needed. They also allowed Blacks to buy food on credit and pay at the beginning of the month. The families that owned these stores were nice and polite, the Doss family and the McVoy's. You could buy a nickel's worth of bologna sausage and crackers and have enough for a full meal.

The main café and feed store was Mrosko's, which served hamburgers, chili, steak, and other common food. They were very accommodating to Blacks, allowing us to buy food on credit and pay at the first of the month. The old-fashioned Icehouse was next to the Iron Gin tracks, where people packed their ice with a string. Once home, it was wrapped in newspaper and rags, and people placed their goods on it to keep it from melting. We also used to go to the ice cream shop that used to be across the street from the library where the old bank was. The man there would put the scoop on the cone, then lick his finger and wipe it around the edge of the ice cream. *Disgusting.*

As I grew up, Mama and I often attended the local movies. In those days, they called it the picture show. Only action and captioning were available. They showed mostly westerns such as Tom Mix, Gene Autry, and a serial movie called the Perils of Pauline. The moving picture theatres were segregated, with lower seating for Whites only. The theatre was located where the current CNBC bank is in Rockdale.

Blacks used to have to pay at the front marquee, then go up the side stairs around back. *We* came in through the back door of the theatre to ascend to the balcony where Blacks were allowed to sit. The balcony was called the buzzards or chicken roost. There were about three or four rows of chairs near the projection equipment and hats. Popcorn was 5 cents a bag, movies were 25 cents, and 10 cents for children under 12. There were no available restrooms for Blacks, only a selected spot behind a building. If you left to relieve yourself and wanted to return to the movie theatre, you had to pay again at full price. The picture shows were located in Rockdale, Caldwell, and Somerville. They were owned by Mr. Matson and his family. We looked forward to the Saturday night movies, for this was really one of the only forms of recreation for blacks. We walked to and from the movies but during the night walks, there was always some fear. Legendary tales told were supposedly about a gigantic shaggy black dog who walked or ran near the Southern Pacific Railroad from early nightfall to after 12 midnight. He was supposedly vicious and would attack people. Fortunately, we never encountered this dog.

Old Hwy 79 once separated the predominately Black part of town and the Fair Park, where they held 19th of June celebrations, track races, baseball, etc. We all went to the same park but had separate areas for our dances, water fountains, and restrooms. Signs citing "Colored Only" or "No Coloreds Allowed" were prominent in most places.

Most Blacks were cooks, common laborers, or picked cotton during those years. There was a place called Batte's farm out from town, and a big truck would pick up Blacks and head to the farm for seasonal work. The horns of the R. L Batte's truck and the camp truck from San Gabriel could be heard at 5am summoning workers. Seasonal farm work like chopping and picking cotton, baling hay, pulling corn, and cutting maize heads were a means of survival. Later in the winter, people went to West Texas to gather crops. Hands were paid 50 cents to $1.50 for picking 100lbs of cotton. Some were able to pick up to 300 lbs daily. The West Texas venture allowed people to make enough money to survive the winter. We had one man, Mr. Ely Floyd, who delivered medical packages to different houses on his bicycle. Blacks had everything we needed *within* our community. As a people, we were usually very resourceful.

At home, Daddy also had a 10-piece orchestra. Both my father and Uncle had bands who often played for the dances (The Moultry brothers' band and the Crayton brothers' band). The Moultry brothers' band consisted of the Samuels brothers (3), the Shields brothers (3), and the four Moultry Brothers. They mostly played for many White-only dances. The Crayton brothers' band was my three Uncles (Percy, Quincy, Tommy) and a cousin, Pee Wee Crayton. They played for mainly country supper, which was an evening dinner meal with music and dancing, located in the country on the north edge of Rockdale. These country suppers were off-limits to Blacks. The bands could play for the entertainment of White folks, but Blacks weren't allowed to attend. We would sometimes ride with Daddy and stay at another Black family's house until he finished playing. One of the parks where these events occurred still stands in Giddings, Texas, right off of Hwy 290.

Blacks sometimes had their own Saturday Night Suppers. Night clubs, cafes and taverns were almost non-existent. The "Saturday Night Supper", sometimes called the "Country Ball was one of the main sources of entertainment. These affairs were held in the homes, mostly in the rural areas, and were only for adults from 21 years and above. To the laborers and field hands, it meant that the back-breaking work of picking and chopping cotton and other forms of manual labor had ended for the week, and it was time to forget about cares and woes, and look forward to a good time at the country supper.

Oft times, in order to get to the ball, some packed their "dress-up" clothes in a waterproof slicker and swam across the shallow creeks, while others rode horseback or came in their buggies and buckboards. Those who could afford a "Model T" Ford would charge 25 cents a "head" to carry passengers to the country supper.

Saturday night also afforded the opportunity to show off a long, lace-trimmed calico dress for the ladies, or velvet "peg-top" with a long-fitted coat below the hips, a white shirt with a tucked or ruffled front and high-heeled shoes for the men. To the chanting of "You get your girl, I'll get mine.... Go to the left; turn that one a loose; And then get another one..." This meant that that it was time to form an old-fashioned circle dance. Or, when the fiddler, the guitarist, or the piano player struck up a sad blues tune or jazz number; the "barrelhouse" dance, Charleston, tap dance, "buck" dance, two-step or "wopsy" were favored. Music was more or less a natural talent, often being played by "ear," or according to one's feelings, cares and woes. There was always someone who could sing or play such tunes as "Red Hot Mama", Maple Leaf Rag", "Baby Don't Cry," "One eyed Woman", "Baby Take-a-me Back" and "C. C. Rider". Words and tunes were often made up to give vent to the feelings and mood of the singer or the crowd.

Food was plentiful. The ladies made hominy in their wash pots to serve with barbecued pork, raccoon, rabbit and opossum, or fried chicken, fish chitterlings, pit feet and pig ears. Desserts were homemade ice cream and cake. Drinks ranged from "red" water, soda water to home brew (beer) made in the homes in stone crocks from Irish potatoes, yeast, salt, and grain. Many families also made "corn liquor", a form of whiskey, in an illegal still from yellow dent corn or rye. Sometimes a card game such as whist or black- jack were played, along with dominoes, or maybe a gambling game behind the woodpile, or smokehouse and often carried on by the light of the moon. These "good times" lasted from nightfall to the wee morning hours. To relieve the drowsiness brought on the long night's celebration, a big pot of black coffee was served to those who stayed over till the morn. Worries were few, and love was abundant. Happiness was genuine at those Saturday Night Suppers.

There were also many singing groups in Rockdale. They played songs like "Should I, Should I" and "Love oh Love, Oh Loveless Love." Whenever Daddy had to go out of town to fill a musical engagement, Mama said Oma G. Burley was my babysitter. The Rev. and Mrs. Burley lived across the road from our house near the railroad tracks. Rev. Burley was one of the community ministers. Sometimes, Daddy would take us with him and would let me sit in the back of the carriage and listen from a distance. Mama and I enjoyed singing together; she sang soprano, and I sang alto. We sang spirituals and a classic number called "Sweet Mystery of Life." Although Mama never had any formal music lessons, she had a special way of playing the piano. Her right hand always carried the melodic tune, while the left had done an odd *bumpity bump.*   Church was the mainstay of the Black community. Pretty much *everyone* went. Each church had their own singing group. The Methodist Church had Ms. Mellie Allen, who played and their singing group. Springfield Baptist Church had its group, Ms. Eva Morgan, Ms. Minnie Mullin, and Ms. Ernestine Mays - pianist. New Hope Baptist Church had a singing group, Ms. Ardie Judy, Lillie Johnson, and Pearlie Davis. Nothing was open on Sundays. Unlike today, people had Sunday dinners at church or home. We had three services a day: Sunday school, morning worship, and night worship. We also had BTU (Baptist Training Union) for young people. There, we had to memorize the Bible, Bible verses, or play Bible games. Sunday was a long day as we went to church early in the morning and stayed until nine or ten o'clock at night. Decades later, my grandson, Jerome, would inherit his great singing ability through Ms. Lille Johnson. The Johnson home still stands in Rockdale. My fun days involved attending church, watching an occasional movie, and sometimes dancing at a little café across the street from our house. We looked forward to playtime on the church grounds. Here, you could buy a big bowl of homemade ice cream for a nickel and sometimes a chicken sandwich. They were delicious! I was never allowed to do a lot of visiting, and I suppose this greatly influenced my personality and characteristics of today. Mama always said, "Seldom visits will always make long-time friends." Mama always had curfew hours for all things. Growing up in a segregated/integrated world was not really difficult for me as a person, for during childhood, I was taught by my parents and developed an inward instinct to beware of undesirable situations. Daddy didn't take much off of anyone, and neither did Mama. They were both outspoken and garnered a level of respect in town from people of all races. Somehow, I learned from my parents the ability to ascertain likes and dislikes, acceptance, and rejection from other races. As a result, my inner self helped me to avoid any difficult situations I might have encountered. Many others also developed the same instincts to avoid trouble.

CHAPTER 5

School Years

My schooling began at the age of five in a segregated classroom at the Rockdale Colored School. The school which bore the name Aycock was opened in 1902. It's building consisted of two rooms furnished with a few battered desks, a bench or two for additional seating, a small table and chair for each teacher, two boxes of crayons, a few erasers, plus a tin water pail and dipper. Two outdoor toilets, one for boys and one for girls completed the facilities. Professor S. S. Adams was Principal and Mrs. Adams was assistant teacher. At the close of springtime in 1903, Professor Adams resigned to accept a position with the War Department at Washington, D.C.

In the summer of 1903, a third room was added to the two- room structure to provide for increased enrollment. At the time, the Board of Trustees elected Bryant Yearling Aycock as principal, Mrs. Lula H. Moseley, first assistant teacher, and Mrs. Minnie Davis Smith (the only graduate of Professor Adams) as second assistant. School opened on October 15,1903. Mrs. Smith passed away in less than two months from illness and was replaced by Professor J. Allen.

The school name was later changed to Aycock after the second Principal of the "Rockdale Colored School," Bryant Yearling Aycock. Mr. Aycock was born in Milam County, December 14,1873. He completed high school in Milam County and was given an award for his academic achievement. He graduated from Prairie View College in 1898. He also taught in Kaufman, Texas. Mr. Aycock was also a co-sponsor of the annual Summer Fairs, held for Blacks and Whites in the 1900s. The fair's main features were exhibitions of livestock, produce, and needlework. Athletic events and other sporting activities were also included, affording opportunities for students and community citizens to be included. In 1903, Mr. Aycock became principal in Rockdale and held this position until failing health occurred in 1921. The school was named for him in 1904. Aycock High School was located on a hill between Third and Pecan Street. Additional history of Aycock and its contributors can be found in the local book, **The Purple Tiger, The Story of Aycock High School 1902-1967 by Susie E. Sansom-Piper. The school mascot was the Tiger and school colors were purple and white.**

My beginning years were most unusual, for it was really the first "known" kindergarten class established by Principal David Solomon Shanks. During these years, there were really no pre-schools or kindergartens, especially for blacks. Professor Shanks scouted the community, selected five five-year-old girls, and placed them in the same room as high school students. Professor Shanks taught school Monday through Friday,was the fish salesman on Saturday., and the Sunday School teacher on Sundays. He also edited the first Black newspaper in the Rockdale area, known as the Brotherhood Eye, which featured news articles about happenings in the black community. Under his administration, four lady teachers taught grades 1-8 and he taught grades 9-11 and the five of us separately. Mrs. Clarissa Allen,

Mrs. Parson, Mrs. Shanks, and Mrs. Grisby taught the students. It was always amazing to me that they were able to handle all of these grades until I began teaching years later.

My school was one of the 5,000 plus Rosenwald schools built throughout the Southern states for Blacks by the late Julius Rosenwald (1862-1932). Rosenwald and his fund were the great impetus that aroused and encouraged southern blacks to dream of a better life through education. was president of Sears, Roebuck, and Company, of Chicago and established the Julius Rosenwald Fund to support the construction of schools for African American children in the southern US. Between 1920 and 1932, the program donated more than $28million in fifteen states and resulted in 534 funded buildings on 475 campuses in Texas. The Rosenwald fund supported not only the construction of schools, but also teachers' homes, and shop buildings in small communities and unincorporated rural communities. Each school had to include an industrial room in additional to the regular classroom. All schools had to stand on at least two acres of land to allow for school gardens as well as playgrounds. There were 4 Rosenwald schools in Milam County, including Rockdale, Davilla, Milano, and Prospect. In addition, there was a Milam County Training School per the Rosenwald inventory listing.

The original Aycock was constructed with lumbar, painted bright orange and white, and was built to accommodate six teachers. It was located on a hill near the Old City Cemetery, and was surrounded by what is now 3rd, Plum, and 4th streets. There were four classrooms, a home economics room, and a large auditorium which could be converted to an additional classroom by closing the folding doors. Each room had a cloakroom in back and there were two book rooms, two miscellaneous storerooms, and an office.

Mrs. Allen was our English, spelling, and reading teacher. She was dedicated. It was a must that you learned excerpts *Thanatopsis*, by William Cullen Bryant, poems of *Invictus, My Task, and Elegy Written in a Country Churchyard.* She taught Shakespeare and you also had to read Greek Mythology. Recently, I learned that she was a novelist, and two of her novels had been discovered in Boston University.

We went to school regardless of the weather conditions or distance. Professor Shanks was a superb disciplinarian. Everyone had to arrive at school at the same time. We all sat in the graveyard across the street to wait until the school bell rang, as we were not allowed to be too early or too late. Being one or the other brought about two or three licks in the hand with his eager strap. We didn't start school until we had prayer and singing every day. Discipline was never a problem, for if you misbehaved at school, you were in great trouble when you returned home.

We were taught reading, penmanship, spelling, and arithmetic. Professor Shanks was a strict disciplinarian. We learned along with the high school students. We had Big Chief red tablets to write in and pencils and writing books. Penmanship to practice writing and spellers to read were part of our daily lessons along with the arithmetic books. The blackboard was still popular and used for teaching and learning. Classrooms were heated with coal or wood-burning stoves.

Any books we had were those whose limitations had expired and had been handed down to the Colored school. Therefore, the books were usually old, ragged, and worn out. The expired books, although usually two or three years old, certainly did not hinder our learning process, for our teacher stressed daily the importance of learning the fundamental skills of math, English, reading, history, and wholesome manners. I have always cherished my early school days, for we were taught many things that were not in textbooks, yet part of our destiny; respect for others, obedience, discipline, and timeliness, to name a few.

At lunchtime, I usually had biscuits and syrup in a tin bucket. Sometimes, I got lucky, and Mama made tea cakes, or I had jelly with bread. Everyone made their own jelly or preserves from fresh fruit. Late summer was dewberry hunting time, so we had fresh preserves and dewberry cobbler.

We always had Monday devotion before class, which meant singing religious, patriotic, and folk songs, along with a scripture and prayer for the week. The same routine was repeated on Friday afternoons before going home for the weekend. Schools and churches coordinated hand-in-hand, so students were encouraged to attend Sunday school and were often quizzed about Sunday morning lessons during the following school week. We were encouraged to attend church on Sundays, and we were given a letter from the alphabet and had to find a scripture beginning with the letter and memorize the same. Professor Shanks had such a great interest in steering his students in the right direction, that he would visit each church on Sunday mornings to see if they were attending Sunday School. On Monday mornings, he would have the students to recite the subject of the Sunday School lesson, and the memory verse that was associated with the lesson.

We celebrated important holidays with a program sponsored by one of the departments. School closings included many functions, such as a primary play, an operetta with full costumes, a three-act drama, a Prom, a Musical, a Talent Show, and all of the graduation ceremonies. These activities gave all students an opportunity to participate in something. We often included adults from the community to participate in the talent shows.

It was during the Professor Shanks era, that Interscholastic League activities began in Milam County. Competition between the two largest schools in the county, Aycock of Rockdale and O.J. Thomas of Cameron (then known as Cameron Colored School) was often very heated. This was also called Fields Day, and was usually held near the close of school. The events consisted of speaking poetry and prose by memory, writing essays, spelling and mathematics contests, music events, and various athletics events. By the time I reached 12 years of age, I was eligible to compete in our county competition for mathematics. My cousin Felix Kendle and I made the team. We won first place, a blue ribbon, in the county. By this time, I was taught a very stiff course of English by Mrs. Clarissa Allen, who was the wife of our local doctor, W.A. Allen. She placed special emphasis on diagramming sentences of Shakespeare, Rudyard Kipling, Walt Whitman, and other famous poets.

I also began taking piano lessons at age 11 under Mrs. Bennie Grigsby. Mrs. Grisby was my first and only music teacher. Her teaching was so intense that by the time I reached 12 years of age, I was able to play for Sunday School at New Hope Baptist Church and later at Springfield Baptist Church. Some of my favorite classical music pieces are Prelude in G, Melody in F, Claire de Lune, Moonlight Sonata, and many others. Her teachings gave me the foundations to later produce winning soloists, quartets, and pianists in local UIL school contests. Three of the Grisby sisters, who were Austin natives, taught music in those schools.

Mrs. Shanks taught us to cook, and her specialty was lemon pies which we baked to sell to the public along with fish sandwiches. Mrs. Shanks was also remembered for making beautiful baskets from armadillo hides. The Shanks left and moved to Austin after some years where Professor Shanks continued to operate his fish business, sell seedling plants, and cultivate a work farm for local fishermen.

In the '30s and '40s, most rural schools were known as Common School Districts and came under the jurisdiction of a county Superintendent. The Superintendent's office was located in the county seat. Usually, there were two or sometimes three teachers who were burdened with the job of teaching at least five grades each. The rural school near my hometown had three teachers and two rooms, one of which was separated by folding doors. They taught through Grade 10, and after completing the 10th grade, students transferred to nearby towns and secured a room to live in while attending school. Students who wanted to secure their high school diplomas had to go to Cameron to complete Grade 11, which was the requirement at this time. There, they completed high school if their parents could afford it. My teachers in my latter high school years included Professors O.E. Wilhite, Powell, Mrs. Allen, and Hogan. All were excellent teachers and provided us with the foundation that enabled us to be college material or make a desirable living after high school.

By 1936, the 11th grade had been added to the curriculum at Aycock, so students who had completed the 10th grade could receive their high school diploma from this school. This change occurred by the time I was ready to finish high school. The Mexicans had their own little school between Rockdale and Milano. There were not a *lot* of Hispanics in town. We all helped each other. There were no indoor toilets in the schools, and heat and air were produced by coal, a wood heater, or raised windows.

Most students walked two to five miles each day as buses were not available. If the weather was bad, parents picked them up via automobile or wagon if they owned one. If it was raining or muddy, this rural area was embraced by the sticky black mud, and chains were required on the auto tires or wagon wheels to travel the roads. Despite limited facilities, hand-me-down books, and challenging travel practices, many students finished high school and college and pursued successful careers.

Dress codes were really different then. I had to wear dresses with bloomers underneath. During the winter months, you dressed for the occasion – no pants for the girls, but cotton stockings and unions or long johns (long-legged underwear) were worn, and high-top shoes. Oh, how I hated those long johns!!! As soon as I had an opportunity to visit the outdoor house (toilet), I would roll them around my thigh during the day and roll them down before going home. Of course, Mama could always tell the difference.

Mama made all of my clothes. She also sewed for people in town. My Mama and three other ladies were the best seamstresses in town. Dresses were often made from colorfully decorated flour sacks they saved. They could take a picture in a catalogue and cut a paper pattern to make the dresses. The dresses would look exactly like the picture. Black people paid the seamstresses 25¢ or 35¢ per dress.

Kids did have pierced ears that were pierced with a hot needle and thread. Coal oil and turpentine were put on your ears after they were pierced to help them heal. We wore the thread in our ears for at least six weeks and turned them every day. My ears were pierced, but the holes were too close to the lobe, and they pulled through. After that, I always had to wear clip-on earrings.

I didn't really have a steady boyfriend in high school. There were several who liked me, but I suppose Harry Jones was the closest to me. I was not allowed to have company because, in those days, you had to be 16 years old before you could "take company." So, our social life involved going to the "picture show" on Saturday afternoons and Jack Wratt's place before dark, a little café that sold candy, hamburgers, chili, and red water. We could play the jukebox for 5¢ and listen and dance to Ella Fitzgerald, Cab Calloway, and others. Our dances consisted of the Jitterbug, Suzy Cue, Trucking, and Twist. There were a number of black businesses in the flats where we lived. Besides Mr. Jack Wratt's, teens could go to Ms. Ruby Ledbetter's, and Mr Fred Foster's to dance. There was Frank Doc Cummings ice cream parlour and barber shop, grocery stores owned by Cebron Sauls, Jim Beals, Withie McKee Sr., and Joe Chandler. These were favorites of children as you could get snacks for 1-5 cents. The stores were also readily available to those who spent long hours working in the cotton fields. Workers could get a hunk of bologna for 10 cents, a can of pork and beans for 10 or 15 cents, plus a 5 -cent soda and some crackers.

Everyone was your parent and watched out for you. Unruly children could be chastised by neighbors, if necessary, or one's parents were informed of any misbehavior, and you "dealt with the consequences" when you arrived home.

I remember Mr. Wash Cartwright. Almost all the teenagers hated him, for he was "always" somewhere around watching and then reporting to your parents if he felt that you were committing a wrong. We always called him the "community police." He was always around when we would visit the lighted church playgrounds some Saturday nights, eat homemade ice cream, cake, and fish sandwiches, and play games. And, of course, on Sundays, church was an important factor and had to be attended.

I was only 15 years of age, but I graduated Salutatorian of my high school class. Graduation was a reverenced moment in our lives. We always preceded this special moment with a Baccalaureate sermon at one of the churches in the community. Then, on the following Friday night, the final graduation ceremonies were held. This was a joyous time, for many gifts were given by various individuals who had received invitations. The settings were usually decorated in a class-selected color. A favorite motto was also displayed on the back of the stage. Caps and gowns were rented and returned to the rental company after usage. We began with ten in our class, but two married early, and the other moved to another town.

• • •

Graduation Address – May 1937

Salutatorian, Susie Emma Moultry

"YOUTH AND TOMORROW"

"Mr. Superintendent, Members of the Trustee Board, Faculty, Parents, Patrons, Visitors, Friends, and Graduating Class of 1937.

We, the Senior Class of 1937, are standing and opening the door to you. We feel highly honored to have the opportunity to welcome you to our graduation exercise. As we are the generation of tomorrow, I have chosen for my subject: "Youth and Tomorrow.'

First, I must ask the question: "What is youth?" Youth is the early part of life that immediately follows childhood or the early part of life from infancy to manhood. Some people define youth as beauty. Youth is one of the most wonderful things that a person can possess.

The youth of tomorrow will be different from that of today. Their form of education will be different. Their moral standards will be higher, and their character will be higher. The youth of today has a greater opportunity than that of yesterday. They have a chance of being educated in free public schools. The youth of tomorrow will have a better opportunity than those of today because of the fact that more forms of education are being added to public high schools. As I gaze into the future, I see better colleges and better public schools, and the education in these colleges and schools will be greatly improved.

Every youth should have some aim in their life. This aim should be to seek for the things that will lead them on the road to success. They should not stoop to low, degrading things that will have an effect on them for a lifetime. Even if the youth does not have the chance of being educated in college, then he should exercise the things that he has learned in high school. This will lead him to his aim, and this will help his aim to be great, and this will help him to be great.

As the youth travels on life's highway seeking for his aim, he should carry these things with him.

"Obedience," which is better than sacrifice. "Helpfulness," which can be exercised at any time; "Truthfulness," which is mighty and will prevail; "Honesty," the best policy that will prevail; "Kindness," the thing that is often worth more than a great deal of money; "Respect" and lastly "Courage" and "Self-Control." These are the things that will carry us on our long journey to success.

There are many things in the world that may keep the youth from progressing. There may be economic conditions as relates to economic conditions or lack of encouragement from homes, communities, and various social institutions. Too often, impossibilities are thrust into our faces, but if we would succeed, we must speak the commanding word "I Will," and this will be done. We must have that "Bulldog Tenacity" to hold on, even though difficulties mount high. We may not have enough money to accomplish everything in life that we desire, but then remember Harriet Stowe's statement; "When we are in a tight place, and everything seems to go against us, then we should never give up, for that is just the time and place that the tide will turn. The darkest hour of the night is just a while before day."

Every youth should have an education because it is an investment that pays richly in reward. The education of tomorrow will be better than that of today. There will be more colleges, and in these colleges, there will be more vocations from which we can choose our jobs.

There is a chance for every youth to receive an education. Every youth should have an "intended" goal in life. This goal should be to become something in life that is worthwhile. Our intended goal may be to write poetry and songs or to teach music, but we must try to make it more elaborate and then make the best of it. We must climb up the long stairway of life. There must be some tears and sorrows and some happy moments, but we must keep striving on until we have reached the very height of our goal. Tomorrow will be better than that of today.

Through our education, we will be able to help other people and to help ourselves. We will be able to meet some of the demands of our society.

If you hope to succeed in life, you must have that bulldog tenacity. Catch hold of your dreams, and don't let go."

• • •

Many graduates in the '30s and '40s had dreams but no hopes of ever attending college. I had dreams of going to Beauty School, for I already knew how to press and curl hair, which only required a straightening comb, some iron curlers, and an oil lamp. I became a "bootleg" hairdresser, and even though I only made 25¢ a head, this was my high school spending change. I became adept at using the straightening comb and curling irons. I used a lamp with a huge metal hairpin across the chimney to hold the straightening comb and curling iron. I was adept at pressing jobs along with croquignole curls. These curls were a way to wave the hair by curling it around metal rods from the ends inward toward the scalp. So, I thought that if I attended Beauty School, I could master the finger waves and Marcel techniques, achieve my state license, become a first-class Beautician, and own a beauty salon.

These dreams were shattered immediately, for money was scarce as "hen's teeth" during that time. My parents could not even afford a six-month beauty course, and no scholarships were available in these early days.

After high school in 1937, the next school term, 1938-39, found me at home with nothing to do. Jobs were scarce. My parents said times were really hard. The threat of World War II was imminent, and so you did whatever work you could find. My neighbor, Vivian, who was attending college, and I chopped weeds on a peanut farm. I also did house cleaning for $1.50 per week. I suppose this was a lot of money for the '30s, for we could purchase a candy bar for 5¢ and a hamburger for 25¢. My mother took in washing and ironing to make ends meet. During this time, you washed clothes with a rubboard. I often watched Mama scrub them, put them in the old black wash pot, boil them, rinse them twice, and put those that needed starch in cooked starch and hang them on the line to dry before ironing them with the smoothing iron the next day. Mama also sewed garments for the public. I kept busy, for I learned to sew, embroider, and cook. I also played piano for different churches sometimes.

Mama was determined that I should go to college. To this day, I don't know how she did it, but she obtained a work-study scholarship for me at St. Phillips Junior College in San Antonio. My tuition would be $11.40 each month, and the balance would be paid through my work/study. Mama felt they could somehow come up with the $11.40 through her sewing and Daddy's blacksmithing yet survive. However, Daddy's income was sometimes uncertain because blacksmithing often depended upon the progress and prosperity of the farmers.

In September 1939, Mama had made my clothes, packed my big old-fashioned trunk, and put me on the Southern Pacific Passenger train en route to San Antonio. A new adventure in my life was beginning. I was 17 years old. St. Phillips was a Junior college where I began pursuing a Business Administration Associates Degree.

At the college, everything was in one building, including the classrooms, the kitchen-dining area, and an elongated room upstairs for the girl's dormitory. Dormitory life was horrible compared to today's dorms. The dorm was a huge monstrosity of a building that stretched from end to end with a long row of cots and a little closet cubicle for privacy. It served as a dressing table, storage, dressing room, or whatever you made it to be. Your trunk was placed at the foot of your bed. We all washed and ironed our own clothes. One large shower and tub was shared by all of the girls. We were one big family.

The food was mediocre. We often ate peanut butter and syrup with two slices of light bread for our Sunday afternoon meal. I was a helper in the kitchen, washing dishes and cleaning the tables after serving. Those who knew how to press and curl hair were the bootleg beauticians. Fortunately, I had a cousin who studied beauty works in high school, so she would help with some of my hair-dressing problems. We also invented our own curling equipment from brown paper sacks. Clothing was limited, and most of my clothes were constructed by my mother. Queen Bae pantyhose were the thing in that day if you could afford a pair. These were much like the nylons with a thick black seam up the back. Otherwise, we often wore anklets with our high heels.

Rules were very tight. Signing in and out was a must! We had curfew hours starting at 7:00 p.m., and no one was permitted to be away from campus after dark without special permission. Social activities were limited to Friday night socials from 7:00 p.m. to 9:00 p.m. and, of course, were supervised. They might consist of a stroll in Lincoln Park and a weekend trip to downtown San Antonio. If we wanted to go downtown in San Antonio, we had to walk. There were no streetlights, and there was only one Black theatre.

We didn't have money, so San Antonio trips were limited to window shopping. We walked from Walter Street to downtown Commerce and Houston Streets. This was mainly Blacks walking this path. We could go to the skating rink on Saturday afternoons, but everyone had to be back on campus by curfew. I don't know what happened if you missed curfew – I never did. Smoking and drinking were considered as bad things to do, yet there were a few girls who always managed to break the rules. I never indulged in *either* habit.

The Episcopalian Church supported the school. Therefore, we all had to attend the Episcopal Church on Wednesdays and Sundays. I played the piano for Sunday school. Everything was supervised. Sometimes Mama would send me a box with summer sausage or bologna, peanut butter, crackers, and sometimes a cake or tea cakes. Mama made the best tea cakes ever! I was only able to go home two times a year, at Christmas and when school was out. My only communication with Mama and Daddy were letters.

My segregated yet integrated experiences began early in my college career. I worked and studied typing and shorthand diligently and tenaciously. We had typing and spelling contests. I won the championship in typing and was the school spelling champion. I was fortunate enough to have my picture in the San Antonio Register. This fete took me out of the "kitchen" and into the office of President Bowden, a rich White lady serving as her personal typist. During those years, the county nurses, who were White, gave all of the immunizations, smallpox, diphtheria, etc., and on those dates, I had to assist with the record-keeping data. I was also an Officer in the Student Council. Somehow, I juggled my job and daily studies. My days were long, and I often did not get to bed until late at night. I worked or studied from daylight to eleven or midnight each day.

I attended St. Phillips for two years, graduating as Salutatorian with second honors and an Associate's Degree in Business Administration. After I finished my first two years, my third year of college found me serving as bookkeeper in the Bursar's Office at Sam Huston College in Austin, Texas (now Huston-Tillotson University). My St. Phillips honors merited me a scholarship to Sam Huston. I continued studying Business Administration, worked hard, and maintained my straight-A average. I also accompanied the college choir. I married at the end of the first semester. In between two daughters and a two-year teaching certificate, I managed to graduate in 1946 Magna Cum Laude with a Bachelor of Science Degree in Business Administration and Education. My college years were happy years in spite of difficult times.

CHAPTER 6

Home Life

During the Christmas holidays, I met the gentleman who was to become my future husband and father of my children, Emzy James "E.J." Sansom. I met E.J. at a church function in the Liberty Hill Community. This was near Mama's sister's house, Aunt Marzella. Her children were going to school to E.J. in Liberty Hill. He taught in the Liberty Hill School, which was in the rural area some ten miles from Rockdale. He was considered to be quite "a catch." He was attractive, neatly groomed, and well-bred in manners. I suppose I was "awe-struck." He was ten years older than me, but most of all, he had an automobile, a rarity among our young men at that time. He also had an eye on my cousin Lessie Mae, but somehow, we became an item. I completed a semester of work at college, but we became so entangled with one another that marriage was the next best thing.

World War II was in focus at the time, and all young men were subject to being drafted into the Armed Services. E.J. often motored to Austin to see me, and we attended the movies or just rode around. We were never interested in attending nightclubs, and neither of us indulged in alcoholic beverages. One Sunday, we attended Springfield Church in the Liberty Hill Community. When offering time came around, E.J. placed 50¢ in the offering basket. The pastor was watching. He looked at him and said, "Is that all you can give?" E.J. never said a word but politely left his seat and retrieved the 50¢ from the basket. I was embarrassed but said nothing. During those days, 50¢ was a lot of money. The average salary for teachers was $60.00 a month, and in rural areas, school only lasted eight months. In later years, I learned that E.J. never bit his tongue when it came to an opinion. You had a choice of proving him right or wrong!

These years were walks in many directions. I finished my second year of college and was 19 years old when E.J. and I married on Valentine's Day 1940 at the Cameron, Texas Courthouse. After we married, we stayed with Mama and Daddy for the next year, and E.J. drove back and forth each day to teach school in Liberty Hill for a few years after we married. Most Black male teachers were coaches and taught other subjects. E.J. taught all subjects at Liberty Hill, including basketball, and served as the school Principal. In those days, you did whatever you needed to do to survive.

E.J. had a large extended family in the Davilla community with eleven or twelve siblings, nieces and nephews, and his parents and grandparents to help. In those days, people had a lot of children, although I was an only child. My husband was a very hardworking man. He taught during the day.

September 7th was a joyful day, for our first child was born. Dr. T.S. Barkley and nurse Sarah Bankston delivered her at the home of my mother and father. She weighed in at seven pounds and expressed her independence at birth, for she absolutely refused to nurse my breast, so she drank Carnation milk. We named her Barbara Sue.

Barbara's paternal and maternal grandparents were greatly thrilled. My Daddy would just sit and hold her and smile and smile. My mom would tend to her daily and made most of her baby clothes. During Barbara's infancy, she developed colic and cried a lot. Mama always had a knack for being the neighborhood doctor long before she became a Licensed Vocational Nurse. So, with her ingenuity, she would take a teaspoon of milk and blow cigarette smoke into it. It worked! Barbara would calm down and soon go to sleep.

Barbara always had tiny, attractive feet, which was a fascination to her grandparents and her Aunt Hattie, who lived in Davilla. Whenever we went to Davilla, Barbara always looked forward to sitting in someone's lap and chant, "Put 'em on, pull 'em off, put 'em on, pull 'em off," talking about her shoes. Of course, they always did just that!

When Barbara was nine months old, we moved to the country (Liberty Hill). This would place E.J. nearer his work, as well as give us a bit more finance to live on. Our first little house consisted of three rooms: two bedrooms and a kitchen. We rented this from Gus Schramm, one of the White farmers in this area. All of this was on the $60.00 per month salary, but E.J. was determined to take care of his family. He taught school during the day and picked cotton in the afternoon after school during the cotton-picking season. He bailed hay and pulled corn during their ripened season. He also raised hogs, chickens, etc., and would always plant a garden. He was dedicated to our little family. I learned how to can vegetables and make jelly and preserves. E.J. kept his 1936 Ford in top condition, for he was his own mechanic! He also made sure that his tires were equipped with chains to combat the black mud road in this area.

That little house in Liberty Hill was nothing special, but I tried to keep it clean and neat for our small family. Our little house was located in a corn, cotton, and maize field with an outside barn where we kept a hog or two. We had an outhouse and a cistern to catch water when it rained. We also had another cistern to get water from the San Gabriel River, which was about a mile from our home. This water was used for drinking and cooking when the big cistern had no water. We had a huge aluminum barrel, which was loaded on a trailer and carried to the river for water each week. We also used this for washing clothes, as a washer/dryer was unheard of at this time.

For heating-cooking purposes, we had a wood heater and a deluxe wood cook stove. To make it warmer during the winter months, we lined the single walls with pasteboard boxes nailed to them and covered them with decorative building paper. We used a "britches" quilt and double blanket for warmth during the winter months. The britches quilt was sewn from several layers of blue jeans. It was heavy and warm, and once beneath it, you could hardly move. On severe rainy days, we always had to keep a bucket or pan nearby to take care of the leaks in the roof.

I often ordered decorations from the Sears and Roebuck catalogue and sewed little decorations to make it homey. We also had a Sears and Roebuck battery radio, which was our weekly entertainment. Our bedroom was equipped with a beautiful bedroom suit from Ribbeck Furniture Store in Thorndale. Our "sitting" room was decorated with Priscilla tri-colored curtains (pink, blue, white) that I had ordered from a Sears Roebuck catalogue. One day, I ordered some beautiful lace curtains to cover the windows in our little front room that served as living room and bedroom. I proudly hung my curtains.

Saturdays were always set aside for grocery shopping and a movie. We motored to Thorndale to purchase our $8.00 weekly grocery bill. My Aunt Marzella, who lived in the area, kept us supplied with milk and butter from her many cows. She also made cottage cheese. In spite of the fact that sugar and several other grocery items were rationed because of the possibility of World War II, we survived!

On Saturday night, we always went to the Dixie Theater, located in Rockdale, which was only 25¢. We always enjoyed the movies, although we had a local doctor and musician who always attended the afternoon matinee and then came back at night and, almost quote for quote, read aloud the captions on the screen and told everyone what would happen in each episode. This was so annoying. One Saturday night after we came home from the movies, my curtains were gone. I was so upset. The curtains had vanished into thin air. In those days, no one bothered to lock doors. A back door and wooden latch were sufficient. A skeleton key, which anyone could buy and use for the front door, was also sufficient. Of course, we lived in the rural area, so we often saw all the field critters, including squirrels, rabbits, opossums, skunks, and field rats. The strange thing was that no doors were open, and no windows broken. Later, I write about *The Case of the Disappearing Curtains*.

Our stay at Liberty Hill was enjoyable; however, there were some traumatic experiences that forever will remain in my memory. First, I had placed Barbara's diapers in the foot tub on the little wood heater to boil to whiteness and took it off for a moment to place additional wood in the heater. Exploratory Barbara, in her walking, fell into the tub. Fortunately, it turned out to be mildly warm, and she did not receive any burns. Barbara always insisted on walking, for she absolutely refused to crawl on her knees. But from that day, she always had a fear of heat to a certain extent and never liked to cook when she got older.

Then, one day in December, the fire in the little room of our three-room house reached its capacity. It put forth its best efforts to emit enough heat to warm the room. Today was a special day for me. My little baby girl is three months old. I am giving her a morning bath, combing her hair, and dressing her in all-white clothes. She falls asleep, so I lay her in the bed under the comfort of my old britches quilt so she will be good and warm. It is time for me to do my daily washing for my precious baby, Barbara. I am going to place her soiled cloth diapers in the foot tub and cover them with boiling water and some ivory soap. I want my baby's clothes to stay pretty and white. Next, I decide to turn on my Sears and Roebuck battery radio and listen to Glen Miller's "White Cliffs of Dover" or perhaps "String of Pearls." While the diapers are boiling, suddenly, the music is interrupted. Stopping and standing perfectly still, I listen to one of the most devastating announcements in my lifetime: "THE JAPS HAVE BOMBED PEARL HARBOR!"

We all sat around listening to the events on our little radio. I can't believe my ears because just yesterday, they announced that the Japanese Ambassador to the U.S. was in consultation with the Secretary of State, Cordell Hull. They were working on a peace treaty. This was frightening, for we recognized that this meant that many of our friends and loved ones would become a part of this disaster.

A thousand thoughts raced through my mind. My husband might have to go to war. I have a classmate in the Navy, and he is at Pearl Harbor. I am thinking and thinking. They bombed Pearl Harbor on a Sunday, which was the day before our normal Monday, due to the time change. Today was December 8th, 1941. President Franklin D. Roosevelt began his most famous Day of Infamy Speech, an excerpt of which follows:

"Yesterday, December 7th, 1941, -- a date which will live in infamy -- the United States of America was suddenly and deliberately attacked by naval and air forces of the Empire of Japan... It will be recorded that the distance of Hawaii from Japan makes it obvious that the attack was deliberately planned many days or even weeks ago. During the intervening time, the Japanese government has deliberately sought to deceive the United States by false statements and expressions of hope for continued peace... As Commander and Chief of the Army and Navy, I have directed all measures be taken for our defense. But always will our whole nation remember the character of the onslaught against us."

There was little change in living conditions until 1941 when war broke out and conditions became more visible. The Japanese had bombed Pearl Harbor; thus, World War II was in full force. Many of the young men in Rockdale were drafted into various branches of the Armed Services, and as they moved about to new surroundings, they noted that living conditions were different and that improvements could be made.

With the possibility of being drafted, E.J. purchased a lot from the late Mrs. Georgia Wells in Rockdale. He then made contact with someone who sold "hot" or "bootleg lumber." Since we were at war, all building materials were rationed for government purposes, and he would buy so much at a time and store it under my parents' home. By 1944, we had accumulated enough lumber to build our first *owned* home.

E.J. was passed over because of the fact that men teachers had become scarce, and it was felt that he was needed in that area. The Colored Schools were part of Common School Districts (CSD) headed by a County Superintendent. Most of the CSD schools were in rural areas. E.J.'s school was in operation for eight months, with three teachers tending through the 10th grade. E.J. drove 10 to 12 miles daily over unimproved roads of black dirt daily.

Many of the citizens on the south side of the tracks were fortunate enough to get electricity and a water hydrant in the yard. However, working conditions still involved dishwashing, maid service, and cotton picking. Walking five and ten miles to attend school or other places was the only way Black people could get around. If you rode the Continental Trailways to another town, you could not sit in the front but were always asked to retreat to the back.

World War II brought about many changes in our lives. Sugar was not the only rationed item. Shoes were limited because of the need for leather. Brother Don worked at a flour mill where they sacked their flour in printed cotton sacks, which contained about one yard each. Mama and I made dresses, shirts, and other things from them for our family. I enjoyed my country life, with the exception of the black, muddy roads. The dark mud was so thick that when it rained, travel became difficult. When it rained, the mud was like glue for your car unless you could afford chains for your car.

So, as the views of returning servicemen changed the views of the world, Rockdale was also to be a part of these changes. Rockdale became a focal point when Marion T. Benson, a Rockdale native who had been drafted into the Navy, was on the ship Arizona when it was bombed at Pearl Harbor. He was a survivor. This particular event served as "a crack in the door" for civil rights, for separatism because of race was soon obsolete in the Armed Services. Eural N. Davis, a returning WWII Vet, also made history for his hometown in the '40s, for he was a member of the famous Drake Relay Team, earning the title of "First Black to travel with a mixed Relay Team."

The bombing of Pearl Harbor in 1941 changed the scenery, for many young men were drafted into the service after the war. Many did not return to their hometown but chose to live in larger cities.

Dirt-laden streets still existed. There was no electricity available across the tracks. The outdoor toilets were still visible. However, a few people managed to secure septic tanks, pit toilets, and outhouses built over a large pit.

· · ·

It was the 9th day of June 1943, a day I will never forget when my second daughter made her debut. I had a bushel of snap beans to can; Eula had different plans. As the pains increased, E.J. decided to rush me to Mama's house in Rockdale, and by 11:30 a.m., Eula announced her arrival. After a week or so, we returned to Liberty Hill to live until our little house was complete. I now had two beautiful little girls who were 21 months apart. I enjoyed making clothes for them, for Mama had taught me the delicate way of using the needle and thread. Babies only wore white when they were very small in the '40s.

After a few years, we built a little four-room house in Rockdale up the street from Mama and Daddy. Our little house in Rockdale was built by Vincente Inocencia and his partner in 1944. Before moving to town from the little house in the rural community, we removed all pasteboard and building paper from the walls and found cut up rags, paper, and whatever behind the window facing. To our surprise, there were my beautiful curtains arranged neatly behind the window facing. We had been missing the lace window curtains for months but never figured out the cause of their disappearance. Finally, we discovered that field mice had cut it down and used it to build a warm, cozy nest for the rat family between the window frames in our Liberty Hill house. Thus, *The Case of the Disappearing Curtains*.

We were so proud of our new home. In the late '40s, under the persistence of the late Frank Owens, a shop teacher at Aycock, sewage became available, and a little later, electricity. So, we had running water, a bathtub, a septic tank for sewage disposal, and electricity. The bathtub was sent from California because, at the time, Blacks were not allowed to buy bathroom sets and commodities in town. Most only had outdoor facilities. Sewage and natural gas were unavailable in this part of town! The ice box was still in existence, and ice "with a string" was still "toted" to homes and stored in a tub or likeness.

We had to purchase an oil cook stove and a wood heater for warmth. As time went by, we added two bedrooms and made our two front bedrooms into a larger living room area. It was well-built. Two walls, wallpapered, and later sheet rock. During the summer months, we had a water cooler stationed in the front living room window. When the electric window fan became available, we replaced the water cooler. The house still stands today and is primarily solid, but it was damaged some years ago from water used to staunch a fire in a neighboring house.

Home life was busy and sometimes tenuous. I was Baptist, and E.J.'s family was Church of Christ. When we married, I went to the Church of Christ with him. E.J. loved to talk to people and would often stop on the street and hold long conversations. I would often send him to the store for milk or bread to finish dinner, and I would be done cooking and ready to eat before he made it back home. He spent long hours shining his well-loved car and his shoes. The car, a Ford, was his favorite. He made sure the girls and I had fine shoes to wear, as he didn't want our feet to hurt or get deformed. We worked hard to make a decent life and be good law-abiding citizens. As teachers, we didn't make a lot of money, but teachers were well respected in the community.

Sometimes, to bring in extra money, I taught piano lessons for 25¢ a lesson to children in our neighborhood. I also did the elderly citizens' hair on Saturdays. I had my own straightening comb and curling iron. It was heated over the stove or through a lamp chimney. I put the curler across the top of the lamp, and when it was hot, I curled and straightened the hair. All of it was 25¢. Before I became a teacher, I had wanted to be a hairdresser, but it was better to become a teacher at that time.

As our girls grew, we were often called upon to help with the extended Sansom family, my parents, as well as other families who had lots of children. Our nieces and nephews would come into town and stay with us to go to school and play sports at Aycock. Sometimes, the girls slept crosswise, five to a bed to make room. I would often get up before school and make homemade biscuits, sew, and fix lunches for our house full. In those days, we all pitched in to help each other whenever we could and wherever help was needed.

By late 1949, little change had been made in public schools. On one occasion, when the distribution of textbooks was issued to the only two public schools, the textbooks were stacked in two columns – new and used. The new textbooks remained at the White school, and the used were for the Black school.

The community faced new changes in the '50s with the arrival of the Aluminum Company of America (ALCOA). Living conditions began to improve, and new families moved to Rockdale. Some of the residents no longer depended on farm labor and domestic labor. Although labor was still on the farms or domestic work was available, a Turkey "Dressing" Factory had also been built near the track, so this provided another form of labor. Aycock School was still functioning in the original Orange Rosenwald Building on Third and Pecan Street. Due to an increased enrollment, two more teachers were added.

There was also the consolidation of rural schools with the Aycock High School (Little Two, Liberty Hill, Tanglewood, Coxes Providence, Sharp, Tracy, Milano, and, in later years, Davilla). Some families moved into the city, and some students were bussed. The community kept the same dedicated and cooperative spirit. Through entrepreneurship and personal contributions, a dedicated Parent-Teacher Association and Band Boosters' Club helped get many needy school items, band uniforms, and general equipment for the school.

The '50s were productive years, for they produced champions in football, basketball, track, band, and academic competition. Segregation still existed, but unknown to many, there was comradeship between White and Black basketball players and band members on both sides of the tracks. Restrooms were still segregated. The back-door dining was yet available, and the theaters still maintained their "chicken roost seats." Common civil rights just did not exist.

Our daughters grew bigger and smarter by the day. Eula, the youngest, often went to school with us as a toddler. As a result, she was two grades ahead of her age. She graduated high school at the age of 15, along with her big sister, Barbara in 1959. They were Valedictorian and Salutatorian of their class, in that order. When the girls graduated, although our salaries were meager, my husband and I managed to save enough to send them both to Prairie View A&M College. September 1959, we had a 1950 Ford. The girls had been given a set of samsonite luggage for graduation, so they packed their suitcases, and we transported them the 89 miles in our 1950 Ford. Their dormitories were assigned according to their majors. They had curfew hours, and even parents could not check them out of the dorm. Barbara, the oldest, was a stellar musician, majored in music, and earned a scholarship to Julliard, although she chose not to go. Eula, the youngest, became a nurse and began a nursing and teaching career in the Dallas area. Each graduated with honors in 1963 in their chosen fields.

As time ventured into the late '60s, many changes in the community began to surface on the south side of the tracks. The city finally laid sewage lines, giving access to indoor plumbing, and natural gas also became available. Families could now enjoy warmth in winter and decent cooking facilities, yet there were still no paved roads on the "other" side of the tracks. The head of the household no longer had to solely depend upon the success of farm crops or travel to south and west Texas to gather crops for provisions during the winter months. The ALCOA plant was not only available to local workers, but many drove to the plant from neighboring towns.

This idyllic setting in Rockdale was soon disturbed by the only known major crime in the '60s, a "shoot out" between the local police and two brothers from the south side of the tracks. The argument was simple and strange, for it involved a dispute with a service station owner over the purchase of gasoline. The end results were the wounding of one of the officers, the death of one brother, and a three-year prison term for the other brother. After serving his sentence, he returned to Rockdale and became a very worthy citizen. He said, "There were so many people in our town who stood up for me and made life easier, for they felt that I was not guilty, but only protecting myself and my family." Once again, "the uniqueness of this city was shown."

After a few years, the school at Liberty Hill closed, and E.J. found work in Borger, Texas. This was far west Texas, so he was only able to come home once a month. Black men went wherever they could to support their families. It was hard during that time. E.J. taught in Borger for several years, making the long trek home every month. While in Borger, he became ill, developing Bells' Palsy. Bells' Palsy is a condition in which the muscles on one side of your face become weak or paralyzed. It affects only one side of the face at a time, causing it to droop or become stiff on that side. His face twisted to one side, and when he came home, his face was droopy, and he talked out of one side of his mouth. After this, he secured a job in Milano, just about ten miles from home. He drove back and forth to school every day while I taught at Aycock.

While the circumstances around us were uncertain, we still made the best of life day to day at home. Barbara and Eula had both married and were working in other cities. We welcomed our first grandchild, Tamara, and E.J. was recovering from a stroke but still teaching in Milano. The little house in Rockdale carries multiple memories of generations. If it could talk, it would tell many true stories. My daughters, Barbara and Eula, grew up here, finished high school, went to college, and married. Three of my grandchildren, Tamara, Cynthia, and Jerome, had their early beginnings in this old house. Two of my grandchildren spent all their growing up, early schooling, high school, and adulthood in this old house.

CHAPTER 7

A New Beginning

After qualifying for a teacher certificate in two years, I was hired as 3rd, 4th, and 5th grade teacher and music teacher at Aycock. My 41-year teaching career had begun. I didn't really feel that I was prepared in a way, and then again, I was manifesting a spirit of fear. It was the beginning of the second semester of the 1943-1944 school year. My entire education prior to my college years had been at this school. I was a hometown girl, returning to my old stomping grounds, and as the biblical statement reads, 'A prophet is without honor in his own country'. The teacher before me had resigned and returned to her hometown to teach. I had been told that the principal preferred out of town teachers, but in this case I was hired on the fact that I had prayed fervently for a job. The previous teacher was a classroom teacher and she also handled all of the musical activities. I did not doubt my ability to teach, but my musical knowledge was limited to my piano training, my activities as an accompanist, and my participation in the college chorus, as well as serving as the musician at some of the local churches.

Within the next few months, Interscholastic league competitions would be held in the county. My job was to train male and female vocals consisting of solos, quartets, and piano solos. The question came to mind, what am I going to do. I didn't know who could sing or who was willing to try. Plenty of females volunteered but there was only one male who was willing to try it. His name was Glen. When I mentioned his name to the high school teachers, they gave little hope and encouragement towards my teaching him to sing. They came back with the statement, 'Why do you want to waste your time fooling with him? He is dumb. He'll never learn. He's just a little country boy who moved to town.' Nevertheless, he was my only male volunteer. The UIL committee always sent a list of songs to choose from according to the classification of your school. We chose *Danny Boy,* which carried the tune of London Derry Air. Meanwhile, I personally studied the dynamics used in singing and judging solo. I prayed fervently for success to come as this was my first venture. The only time we could rehearse was before or after school, and during lunch. There were no special time periods set aside for rehearsals.

Ultimately, Glen won first place in the county. This entitled him to compete in the District competition thus preparing him to challenge all State participants for the gold medal in male solo competitions. To everyone's surprise, Glen brought the bacon home! He was my very first gold medal winner!

From that day forward, Glen had taught me a valuable lesson which carried me through all of my teaching experiences for the next 40 years. " Never say what can't be done! Believe that you can and you will!" Glen graduated from school that year. He enrolled in college in Austin choosing chemistry as his major. From there he went to the armed services and after completing his tours, enrolled in the University of Minnesota receiving a master's degree in chemistry. He later became the first black to be hired in his field in Houston Texas Energy Department. During that time he also studied and received a Doctoral degree in Chemistry and was immediately recruited as a space scientist with NASA at Kelly Air Force Base in San Antonio. He remained there until his retirement. In between these accolades, he wrote and published many scientific papers became an inventor, and was inducted into the National Hall of Fame for Inventors.

Glen is one of the students that stands out foremost in my mind for through him, I learned to believe, aspire, achieve and never say it can't be done. He also left a lasting impression with me that one should never label children as dumb, but search for their best capabilities. Everyone has a given potential. As an educator, it is our duty to find and develop it. Thus was the beginning of my rewarding career. Through the lesson of perseverance from Glen, I wrote the first and only school song, which is still sung at Aycock Reunions to this day.

SCHOOL SONG "Dear Old Aycock High School"

Dear Old Aycock High School

Of the Purple and White

Dear Old Aycock High School

For you, we will always fight.

Dear Old Aycock High School

Keep your colors flying,

Let them be our guiding light.

Dear Old Aycock High School

For you, we will always fight.

Dear Old Aycock High School

We're in love with you.

Dear Old Aycock High School

Say you love us too.

Keep your home fires glowing,

In your heart so true,

Dear Old Aycock High School,

We're in love with you.

We're in love with you!

Composed in 1943

By Susie E. Sansom

As I settled in to teaching, I became accustomed to the ways and expectations of the Aycock school to a certain extent. In our separate school, we had to entertain the members of the School Board each year with a fabulous dinner cooked by our Home Economics teacher and her students. It was my duty to furnish the entertainment. All of our faculty were in attendance, but we could not dine with the Board. Instead, we had to remain seated in a specified area, and after the ceremonial dinner and the departure of the School Board, we could dine.

There was still the traditional belief by the White race that all Black teachers were inadequately prepared to teach. So, during the summer months, our faculty attended summer school, and soon, the majority of our faculty had obtained a master's degree in some field. (This will be further explained in a future chapter.) I had completed my Bachelor's Degree in Business Administration and Elementary Education and later a Master's Degree in Business Administration-Education. I then returned to school to become a Certified Counselor.

During this time, all programs and athletic activities were separate. We had no special equipment, only hand-me-down textbooks, chalk, and blackboards. Various programs, talent shows, dramas, etc., were a means to secure the finances needed for supplies for our school. We even raised enough money to purchase a motion picture machine and show movies on Friday and Saturday nights.

We did not have a gym. The students played on a lime-outlined dirt basketball court and held our track meets at the city park in the afternoon, usually on a Friday. Only boys played the game during these years. A small fee was charged to neighborhood people who attended. We had access to the White High school football stadium on Thursday or Saturday nights or on a Friday night when it was not in use. We had hand-me-down football uniforms, and after school, the home economics department would spend time mending them after a game. Our school also produced outstanding students, academically and athletically. These were but a few things that existed in the traditional Black school before integration.

The school was an "entertainment center" for the entire community. They always celebrated the holidays with a special nighttime program. At the end of the school year, there were elementary, junior high, and high school functions to provide entertainment. With the support of the parents and the community, no child was left behind. During the early '40s, when many other Rhythm and Blue Singers emerged, it seemed that Aycock Schools also began a quest for Fame that would extend through the next 30 years. The teachers and students who matriculated there made names for themselves through perseverance and determination.

Community, love, and cooperation were still prevalent. And oftentimes, funds were obtained from the school through a combined school and community talent show. The Parent Teacher Association was headed by Miss Clemmy Goins. For many years, there was an oddity to her willingness to work in the community, for she had no children of her own. Her home was the rooming place for teachers who came from other towns to teach at Aycock. This era is often known as the Decade of Champions for Aycock, for there were state winners and literary events, football, basketball, track, band, debate, and home economics. It was also the beginning of the Aycock Band under the leadership of Theo Howard. Their performances were amazing because they consisted of 6th, 7th, and 8th grade students. What is little known is that many of the students from Rockdale High would visit the Aycock Band Hall and practice with this little band. This was the beginning of integration in the Rockdale Schools. Long before the Civil Rights Law, the students were unofficially integrating themselves.

These same ideals were followed by students on both sides of the tracks on the basketball courts as well. During this era, Common School Districts were eliminated by the Texas Education Agency. High school students from Milano, Griffin Chapel, Thorndale, Sharp, Tracy, Gause, and Leo, which was between Lexington and Rockdale, were affected. Aycock moved to a new school campus in 1954 and remained there until final integration in 1967. It served black students from Rockdale, Milano, Thorndale, Lexington, Gause, Tanglewood, Minerva, Davilla, and the communities of Liberty Hill, Coxes Providence, and Griffin Chapel. This move provided more action by way of attendance of school functions in the community. Many students from both campuses, old and new, brought a measure of pride and fame to their communities through their endeavors.

Meanwhile, *my* world became more integrated because the Superintendent upgraded my position to half-day classroom instructor, school secretary, and bookkeeper.

In those days, we had to be "jacks of all trades" and innovative enough to fill in wherever or whenever necessity called, which meant you were not only a classroom teacher but the school secretary. You suddenly became a public speech trainer for UIL activities, a five-point music teacher, training your students to sing in quartets, solos, male and female piano competitions, or drama director for closing activities. You were also a producer of community talent shows, etc. You worked hard! You worked! But one thing stood out. You had the respect of the students and the support of their parents and the entire community.

It was in this new chapter during the '50s when counseling became prominent in the public school system. I found myself again in an integrated situation, for I was designated to assist the White counselor for the school system in conducting all of the testing programs. As I went to college to obtain my counseling certificate, it soon became my job to administer and interpret all scholastic tests that were given at our school. All of these duties assisted me later when the schools became integrated.

During the summer months, I attended Prairie View University and obtained my Master's Degree in Administration and Elementary Education. Because of my segregated-integrated position in the testing programs, I also acquired a Counselor Certification and qualified for two summers of National Science Foundation Programs in the field of mathematics. Somehow, my education ventures always helped me to work directly or indirectly with my White counterparts, so perhaps I can say that integration was not as difficult for me as it may have been for some of the other teachers with whom I worked.

While watching the movie "Radio", based on a true story about an African American student who is mentally disabled in a racially divided town, I was inspired to write about Ed. This was my ninth year of teaching and I had a new assignment. I was placed in the Jr. High and High School departments to teach Economics, American History, and seventh and eighth grade mathematics, along with handling all of the musical activities like I had in the previous years. Ed, who was a junior in high school was not retarded as referred to during that time; however, he was labeled as having some mental disability due to his emaciated physique and mannerisms. He was very tall, lean, and looked as though he was suffering from some form of malnutrition. Ed lived with his mother and stepfather, and in later years, I was told that his stepfather was very abusive. For some reason, God always seemed to place those students who were taunted and ignored by others under my wings. I began to take an interest in Ed for I discovered that in spite of his appearance and the label that had been placed on him, he was very capable of learning. Ed was small in stature, quiet and mannerable, quiet in speech, and possessed an humble spirit. He graduated from Aycock in 1955 and after his parents' demise, moved to Temple,Texas. Like Radio, Ed had no particular work skills, but was encouraged to apply at the famed Scott & White Hospital. In 1957, he began working on the job transporting patients from their rooms to x-ray diagnostics. A few years later, he was transferred to nursing services to receive in-service training.

Through his studies, he became a certified nursing assistant in the orthopedic ward. In 1977, he was selected Employee of the Year. A patient had written a letter to the hospital and according to excerpts from the hospital bulletin, wrote as follows. *Following surgery, I was fortunate enough to have been taken care of by Mr. Ed X. He very quietly persuaded me to do whatever needed to be done. This man goes about his daily work so quietly and efficiently that you don't even know he is there. ...I think this would be a better world if we all put the kind of compassion and quality in our work that Ed does in his.* Ed remained with Scott & White until his retirement. Through patience and perseverance, Ed proved (like *Radio)* that you can make it if you try.

"Conquest is not always measured in battles fought and won, but through perseverance and patience, coated with tenderness and love."-Susie Piper **(Excerpts from Ebony Etchings 1982)**

The segregated-integrated years were eras of many changes in my life. I began as an elementary teacher at the Aycock School and moved up the ladder to middle school and high school teaching. I taught a variety of subjects, including typing, shorthand, bookkeeping, history, social studies, chemistry, and music. We had a large number of Aycock students who went on to make great contributions to society with their work ethic, determination, and special talents.

Four young men, Eural Norman Davis, Harry Wayne Jones, Johnnie Lee, and Blanche Talley were gold medal winners at the State Interscholastic League Activities held at Prairie View A&M College. They became well known for their unusual singing talent.

In 1947, the Fiftieth Texas Legislature established a committee to study educational reform in the wake of a legislative deadlock over the passage of a minimum salary law for Texas public school teachers. This committee was later named the Gilmer-Aikin Committee after Representative Claud Gilmer and Senator A.M. Aiken, Jr.

My starting salary was $75.00 per month, and according to many rumors, Black teachers' salaries were different from White teachers until the Gilmer-Aikens Bill was passed. When the Gilmer-Aikens law was initiated in the Texas Education System, we learned that, in fact, there were higher salaries for White teachers, even though they had less education than their Black counterparts. After this law, the salaries became better. In later years, we were told that there was a Black/White salary scale. Unfortunately, disparity between blacks and whites, men and women when it comes to equal pay still exists in some areas today.

After a 20-year adventure in my segregated-integrated world, things began to fester like a sore boil, and my segregated-integrated world slowly disintegrated into a completely integrated world. Then, the next three years began to change.

CHAPTER 8

The Handwriting on the Wall

I n 1892, the Plessy vs. Ferguson decision set the legal precedent for the concept of "separate but equal," which had applied to the schools in Southern states since then. In most cases, the schools were far from equal, but throughout the South, they were indeed separate. So, for the next 58 years, southern schools remained segregated, supposedly equal, yet unequal.

The handwriting on the wall began to appear when, in 1950, the Supreme Court decided the case Sweatt vs. Painter. The case had been brought by Heman Sweatt, an African American who qualified to attend law school at the University of Texas but was denied admission because of his race. In response to Sweatt's lawsuit, the State of Texas established an all-Black Law School in Houston and argued that he could attend that school. The Supreme Court found not only tangible inequalities between the two schools but also "intangible" inequalities in prestige, faculty, reputation, and administration. Ultimately, the Supreme Court ordered his acceptance to the UT School of Law. This was the beginning of the judicial acceptance of the idea of racially separate treatment in education as inherently unequal. In response to Sweatt's lawsuit, the State established Diversity and Outcomes in Higher Education Symposiums.

In 1954, we moved the Aycock School into a modern and well-equipped brick building. This was a dramatic and pleasing adventure, for we had left the traditional orange Rosenwald schools with its coal-operated pot-bellied heaters and outdoor toilets. One of the early sports was basketball, which was played in the afternoon, usually on a Friday, on a lime-outlined court. The first band was organized in 1952. Within three months, the band director had produced a band with 6th, 7th, and 8th grade students that became the envy of any bands throughout the state. The White students would slip away from their homes in the afternoons and practice with this band. Their school won championships in the literary, music, and athletic fields. In 1953, a new modern Aycock School was erected. It was only ten years old when integration began.

Although we were modernized, there was still unrest, for previously, in 1951, the father, Oliver Brown, of elementary school student Linda Brown had filed suit against the city of Topeka, Kansas, because his daughter could not attend schools near her neighborhood. Linda Brown was a little African American girl attending third grade at a public school in Topeka, Kansas, in 1951. She lived a few blocks from a White elementary school, but when her father attempted to enroll her in the neighborhood school, his request was denied. As a result, Linda Brown traveled about a mile every day to get to the nearest Black elementary school. In 1951, Ms. Brown's case was heard by the U. S. District Court of Kansas, but they ruled in favor of the Topeka Board of Education.

The case was appealed, and it went to the U.S. Supreme Court in the fall of 1951. It was tossed around for the next two years, along with similar cases from Delaware, Virginia, and South Carolina. In 1953, the Supreme Court heard it again. Thurgood Marshall, who was the first African American Supreme Court Justice, argued for Brown and the National Association for the Advancement of Colored People (NAACP). This case, though prolonged, opened the doors to desegregation in public schools. Brown vs. the Board of Education would become the landmark case that resulted in the desegregation of public schools and led to the abolishment of the separate but equal school system in 1954.

On May 17, 1954, the U.S. Supreme Court rendered its decision: state-sanctioned segregation of public schools was a violation of the 14th Amendment and was, therefore, unconstitutional. By this time, Linda Brown was in middle school. Segregationists across the South sprang into action to prevent the implementation of public-school integration. In some states, the legislature passed state laws to uphold segregation, which then had to be challenged in court by the federal government one by one, thereby delaying the day when Black children would be admitted to White schools. Some White segregationists formed councils to fight against desegregation. One of the most dramatic scenes surrounding school desegregation occurred in Little Rock, Arkansas, in 1957, when a White mob surrounded and screamed threats at nine Black students and blocked them as they tried unsuccessfully to enter their new school for the first time. President Eisenhower ended up calling in the National Guard to protect them. There was much fear, apprehension, disillusionment, and chaos existing throughout the South because of this court order. Even in our small town of about 5000 inhabitants, fear existed.

The handwriting on the wall continued from 1954 through 1964, and many, many things began to happen. These were years of uncertainty, insanity, hatred, unrest, and the loss of many lives. In 1963, President John F. Kennedy, was assassinated. The Supreme Court, the law of the land, had firmly and emphatically declared that equality in education was non-existent and that all schools in the country must be integrated to achieve equal educational opportunities. Southern states declared emphatically that they would not accept the new rulings. The faces of inequality even spread to the west coast and the middle eastern states. Rockdale waited as long as legally possible before complying with the fullness of the law, which also included the integration of public facilities and eating places. Literally, Rockdale played with the edict twelve years or until it became a "must" or "suffer the consequences". In the midst of waiting, some confrontations and arrests were made when attempts were made to enter the Dairy Queen and several of the public swimming pools.

The desire and pressure for "civil rights" was the great issue at this time. Rioting, burning of churches, and murder of innocent children ensued across the country and in southern states. Rosa Parks refused to move to the back of the bus, thus giving her the distinguished title of *Mother of Civil Rights*. Martin Luther King Jr.'s leadership began in the cause for justice and equality and his staunch declaration that "segregation is on its deathbed." Dogs and fire hoses were used to quell demonstrations. The list goes on and on. However, very little of these brutal actions were in the central Texas area. It is gratifying to know that portions of Texas did not emulate her sister states, although she was slow in obeying the law of the land. The most significant happenings during this time were the assassination of President John F. Kennedy in 1963, followed by the assassination of Dr. Martin Luther King Jr. in 1968.

These events bring to mind Mrs. Lathan, another White associate in my segregated-integrated world. Mrs. Lathan was a counselor from the county who came to our school twice a month. I always worked with her on whatever project she presented, but to this day, I have never really understood her purpose for being there. I somehow felt that this was a job made for her until her final retirement years. I, for some reason, had an instinctive intuition that she was very prejudiced, through just noticing her overall attitude toward Black children and generally around adults. She sauntered into our school, looking down her nose with an air of superiority.

On the day President Kennedy was killed, our school, adults, and children were in tears. When Mrs. Lathan came that day, she was just the opposite. She seemed to have been elated and had an expression of gladness. At this moment, I had a fearful feeling for her, for the teachers who were in the office at the time of the announcement noticed her actions and became angry. I suppose she recognized this, for suddenly, she packed her briefcase and "got out of there." I have always wondered what would have happened if she had remained for the rest of the day.

President Kennedy had initiated the call for "civil rights" before his assassination. President Lyndon B. Johnson expressed the desire for the passage of this bill, noting that it was a cause that Kennedy had fought diligently for. So, he met with Congress days after the assassination and said, "No memorial oration or eulogy could move or more eloquently honor President Kennedy's memory than the earliest possible passage of the civil rights bill." On July 2, 1964, President Johnson signed the Civil Rights Act, which outlawed all major forms of discrimination, including in public schools and workplaces, and against racial and ethnic minorities and women.

Title VI, 42 U.S.C. § 2000d et seq., was enacted as part of the landmark Civil Rights Act of 1964. It prohibits discrimination on the basis of race, color, and national origin in programs and activities receiving federal financial assistance. As President John F. Kennedy said in 1963, "Simple justice requires that public funds, to which all taxpayers of all races [colors, and national origins] contribute, not be spent in any fashion which encourages, entrenches, subsidizes or results in racial [color or national origin] discrimination." This legislation at the beginning of integration required the desegregation of public schools and universities if entities wanted to receive federal funds.

Webster defines civil rights as "the rights to personal liberty established by the 13th and 14th Amendments to the United States Constitution and certain constitutional acts." Before 1964, this definition was only words written in textbooks to be read by America's students and practiced only by a specific race of people. After the end of slavery, although the Fifteenth Amendment gave the right of black men to vote, it was common knowledge that this excluded blacks. States were slow to implement the right to vote until Lyndon Baines Johnson signed the Voting Rights Act into law in August 1965. Our late President Johnson said, "The right to vote is the basic right without which all others are meaningless." An integral part of the Civil Rights Acts included the right to vote. During this era, voting for individuals to occupy certain offices was relegated only to one race of people. One may readily ask the question: why?

Many Blacks did not vote because of economic conditions. During those days, many had to follow seasonal work in the cotton fields just to survive. Many children did not get to enroll in school at the beginning of the year because of this work schedule. As a result of this migrant work status, voting and educating oneself about candidates were not a paramount concern in the community because people were trying to eke out a day-to-day existence in the early '50s.

The bill had immediate results. At the time, a poll tax was required in three states (Texas, Alabama, and Virginia). When people did vote, the $1.75 poll tax, the amount required to register, had to be paid. That money was often hard to come by Considering we cut and styled hair for 25 cents on weekends to make extra money, five times that amount to vote was a lot. This amount could feed the average big family for many days back then, and besides, they had to save money for the winter months. In some cases, employers would pay the tax for black voters and dictate for whom they should vote. As a teacher, we had no choice but to register with the $1.75 fee, for we were expected to cast our vote. Oft times, we were, as teachers and employees of the school district, "told" who the "preference" was by the "powers that be" and were expected to cast our vote accordingly. Once in the voting booth, however, we cast our ballots for our candidates of choice. Most people did not have adequate transportation or news media to learn about the importance of voting. So, efforts or knowledge had to be passed on by word of mouth, schools, churches, and other organizations that existed on the other side of the tracks. Though many became eligible for voting due to the aforementioned factors, few actually followed through with the voting process in my hometown. Eventually, their cohesive vote produced the first Black council member of the city of Rockdale in 1978, Freddie Gray, and every election since that time has produced additional Black council members.

The next three years brought many changes to this community. Numerous statements, opinions, and questions came from both sides of the tracks concerning how Rockdale would deal with the upcoming integration changes. We never really had any other major undesirable happenings in my hometown, but there were always the questions of Why, When, How, Where, and just *What* will happen.

"When will we integrate the schools?"

"I don't want my child to cross the tracks in front of those beer joints."

"I hope my child will have only White teachers in the future."

"I feel so sorry for those little Black children."

"How will they get to the schools?"

… and on and on.

CHAPTER 9

The Ball Begins to Roll

For me, a small-town Black teacher, integration had its muddled beginnings in 1964 when a portion of the high school was moved to the all-White school. Three years went by before the integration process was completed in Rockdale. Two neighboring towns, Milano and Thorndale, had quietly integrated the year before. The community of Davilla students were transferred to the town of Bartlett, which was only eight miles away. There was apprehension, fear, misconception, and backwards beliefs among all people.

Whites resented what was about to take place. It was difficult to go shopping in our small town without encountering a questionnaire or biased statement. I often went to the flower shop to buy small trinkets and flowers. It truly got on my nerves because the lady there was so nice-nasty, as I called it. This meant that on the surface, she pretended to be nice, but underneath was a very visible, nasty, ugly spirit. Every time I went in, she smiled and said, "Oh, I feel soooo sorry for the little 'nigra' children, Susie. Do you think they will have decent clothes to wear up there at the school? Will their folks have enough money to keep them in school?" And she would shake her head and click her tongue with pity. I would just look at her. "I'm sure they will be fine," I'd say and go about my shopping.

Deep within, my feeling was, "Why feel sorry for us now? We have survived the shackles of slavery. We have lived within the wall of the Jim Crow laws. We are survivors!" But I nonchalantly went about my way. It seemed as though the old town patrons enjoyed flashing the N-word to you as they raised their questions, but, through the years, we had learned to ignore or tune people out unless it became too offensive or insulting. One day, she saw two little girls passing by on the sidewalk. "Oh my," she exclaimed. "Aren't they just the cutest little things, and just look at their little dresses? I wonder where they got those." I just smiled to myself, ignoring her ignorance. Whatever we didn't have, we knew how to make, and no one would go without.

Others said, "I hope they close the Black school because I don't want my child crossing the tracks by those beer joints." A preposterous idea evolved. The Whites simply expressed that it would be best to close down a practically new building because they preferred that their children would never have to cross the tracks to go to school. Still others expressed fear of Black children playing with White children, and at the same time, some Blacks said, "I'm glad my child is going to the White school. They won't ever have to go to school to a Black teacher, and they will get a better education." The theory was that Black teachers would become obsolete. Whites wondered if a Black teacher could do a good job or if we were qualified. As teachers, we were caught in the middle. I watched and waited to see how it would all play out.

In the midst of this, the remaining Class of 1965 quietly prepared for the final graduation ceremonies at Aycock. The class of 1965 was the last 12th-year class to march across the stage and receive their high school diploma at the old Aycock High School. It was an emotional time, for this meant that the high school that had produced so many outstanding Black citizens throughout the world was shutting down. Eleven seniors and twenty 8th-grade students completed the final chapter. Strangely, the theme was "Image of Tomorrow". The high school departments of Rockdale and Aycock were fully integrated during the 1965-66 school term. The 6th graders and one teacher were transferred to Middle School. Two Aycock teachers were transferred to the High School. Students of this community in grades 1-8 remained at Aycock. In 1967, I served my last year in the Aycock segregated school as head teacher for a "sprinkling" number of pupils and teachers.

Fifty-one children in grades 1-4 chose to remain at Aycock. The Principal, O. E. Wilhite, and four teachers, Frankie Moore McDonald, Artie Mae Williams, Lucy Bell Battle, and I, remained to dissolve what was once Aycock High School and write the final chapter of a great school. Ruth Howard would serve as secretary. As head teacher, it became my duty to transfer all books, trophies, and uniforms and distribute all memorabilia, equipment, etc., to the necessary specified (elementary, junior high, and high school) campuses. The building, which served as Band Hall, Library, and Agriculture Department was moved to the junior high campus. This served as the junior high band hall and special education room for that campus.

The year dragged slowly by. There was a strange and indescribable quietness on the campus with the few remaining. Near the end of the year, it was announced that remaining Black students (with parental approval) would have "Freedom of Choice" to attend the White elementary school. This meant that any student at Aycock, from grades 1-8, could attend Rockdale Elementary or Middle School on the north side of the track. The 7th and 8th grades would be transferred to Rockdale Junior High.

In May of '67, a picnic marked the closing of a chapter of history for a school which had its beginnings in the early 1900's. Its 65-odd-year history had concluded. The school that began in a Masonic Hall with 3 teachers and grew to a prestigious school with 18 teachers. This school had garnered state championships in football, basketball, band, and other UIL activities. It was a school that produced nurses, sculptors, x-ray technicians, college professors, college presidents, and many other accomplished personnel. A new era of life in and out of the classroom began for me and many others. A final barbeque picnic was held under the huge oak trees on the North side next to the new Aycock building or directly in front of what is now called Moultry Park, named for my father (Julius Moultry). We huddled there to pay homage and bid farewell to a great school. At the time of this writing, there are only five living remaining teachers from the former Aycock High. The building still stands unused today on the grounds of what is now Moultry Park. This was a prelude to a new beginning of my Seventeen Years in the Black Room, years that were filled with stress, emotions, accolades and rewards, and finally compliments for a job well done.

The end of 1966 into 1967 ushered in the integration of the Milano, Milam County Schools. My husband, who was teaching at the Black school in Milano during this time, had been terminated from his job as elementary principal. He had been the principal of the Milano Elementary School grades 1-8 until the end of 1966. Milano, like many schools in surrounding areas, *eliminated* all of the Black men teachers. A unanimous decision in the district where E.J. taught was that no Black men would be hired in the integrated schools. Many of the Black male teachers, like E.J., were considered undesirables to teach *White* female students. These highly educated men lost their jobs and often moved away from their families to teach elsewhere. They hired one Black female, and the rest were let go. Once again, E.J. had to leave our area to find work. Fortunately, he found employment as a math teacher in a school in Harris County or the Houston area. This permitted him to return home on weekends and stay with his sister during the week.

In 1967-68, obedience to the Civil Rights Act was completed. The school term of 1967-68 was a year of perseverance, endurance, and survival. Mixed emotions continued to grip the small town of Rockdale. This was in both communities. The year was challenging at home and school. I felt like a guinea pig. As time went on, only a few of us would survive the integration years and go on to have successful long careers. Initially, only one teacher was moved from Aycock. She only lasted six weeks before having to resign because of the pressure which created extreme stress. After integration, we all had to continuously prove ourselves.

Essentially, when we were moved to the integrated school, we were all split up. There seemed to be a concern about the Black teachers congregating and the students as well. We were assigned the challenging classes and students. Professor Wilhite retired and moved to Fort Worth for a short while to manage Masonic Apartment Complexes. Laura Petty and Mildred Lovelady had already been assigned to high school in 1965-66. This left me to find my way in the new landscape a year or two later. These happenings changed the general face of community life on the other side of the track, but the real essence lies in the fact that the "uniqueness of getting along" still remains.

The Black teachers began to do a movable dance that I called the "Shuffle," for there was definitely a shuffle for jobs or to hold a job. In 1964-1965, a husband-and-wife team, our Band teacher and Home Economics teacher, the Timmons, made their move by accepting work in the Temple Public Schools as Junior Band Instruction and Supervisor of Elementary Curriculum. This, in later years, proved to be a loss to our schools and a plus for the North Texas Public Schools. This couple moved to North Texas as High School Band Director and the Home Economics teacher went on to earn her Ph.D. in Education and was Superintendent of the Fort Worth Schools. Although now retired from public schools, she is now a national analyst in testing programs and travels worldwide. Other teachers who had reached retirement age were retired. Those who maintained homes in other cities returned to their hometowns, and those who had homes in our city were retained as faculty members until the integration process was completed. Black teachers were only retained if they owned property in Rockdale. The remaining faculty members who were boarders had to seek employment elsewhere.

Two faculty members from our school were sent to high school, and one faculty member to middle school to teach 6th grade English. There was a struggle for survival as a faculty member. Pressure was on the faculty to integrate, and the stress took a toll on some teachers. There was in-fighting and severed relationships between faculty. Now, our school wasn't perfect. There had always been some small-town scandals and gossiping at times, like the time we had to lock a teacher in the library because the wife of a man she had taken up with threatened to come to the school and beat her. Another tragic incident and scandal happened when another teacher had a family member murdered by a gay lover in a murder-suicide tragedy. The stress of the changes coming were taking a toll on many. Our music teacher remained one year before returning to Houston. One teacher underwent so much pressure in the middle school that she suffered from illness and had a nervous breakdown. As a result, she never returned to the classroom.

Laura Petty, when transferred to the high school, was at first denied a position in her field of biology and was given physical science and remedial math courses, which were considered to be for slow learners. The first year was hectic. The majority of Blacks, four Whites, and Hispanics were placed in these classes, but Laura made them learn, so to speak. By her account, for the next four or five years, she consistently requested a biology position but was always denied. Even after Mr. White, the biology teacher, left, Laura was still not assigned to Biology until two more years after his departure. She was an excellent teacher, and her students learned and excelled.

Flora Mack spent a short while as 6th grade English teacher at junior high. She was the first to go to the Junior High, but she was only there for a few short months before she became ill. She died suddenly right after integration.

Lucy Battle was assigned originally as a "floating" elementary teacher. This meant she moved to any room where she was needed. She taught elementary in the Aycock schools and was outstanding with children. Like many of us, she was assigned a position that did not fully utilize her skills with elementary-age children. In later years, she was finally given a 1st-grade classroom. Before her retirement, she emerged as one of the "best 1st-grade teachers" Rockdale schools ever had.

Mildred was given choral music but only remained at the High School one year before relocating.

Artie Williams and Frankie Moore were assigned to Special Education in the old band hall, which was moved to the campus. They remained in teaching positions with the Special Education departments until their retirement. A sprinkling of a few other Black teachers came after integration, but the transition from Aycock to the Rockdale integrated schools was the most difficult and paved the way for later transitions.

We felt denigrated or were somberly reminded of the old myths of years gone. Some whites assumed that Black teachers were not well learned, had a poor foundation, could not function, or fit in an integrated classroom. So many false perceptions!!!

CHAPTER 10

THE BLACK ROOM

Late August 1967 began the start of a new job and a new way of life, for it was then that I began my years behind the Black Room. My teaching career began at the Rockdale Junior High School. A lonely Black teacher among fifteen White teachers, the only Black teacher on this faculty of seventeen (including the principal).

Of the teachers who moved to the Rockdale schools, four of us held Master's Degrees, two in Elementary Education, one in Administration, Education, and Counseling, and one in Biology. Few White teachers had obtained Master's Degrees at that time, and they were attending extension school from Prairie View A&M, an institution that was a historically Black university. It was ironic because it formerly did not meet their *approval*.

My first experience in the classroom was not really as a teacher but as a figurehead of experimentation. I like to think of the late Ernie L. Lawrence as the "grand old principal," for in his way, he made every effort to make integration work. He introduced me to the staff, made his "pep talk," and had his secretary, Irene Speer, to pass out the assignment rolls. I was to report to a room in the basement of the old junior high building. This building had formerly been the high school until the new one was built.

Principal Lawrence told me that there were a lot of students who were behind in their studies, so they were adding a new curriculum. I was assigned to teach *all* subjects, some of which they gave the title of "supervised study." He told me, "What I want you to do is map out a plan whereby they can improve or be brought up to the level where they should be." "Here I am," I said to myself. "I have a Bachelor's Degree in Business Administration, a Master's Degree in Administration and Elementary Education, and a Counselor's Certificate. And I have to teach supervised studies. Now Susie… you have never given up. Prove Yourself!"

The search was on. I checked educational catalogues, stores, and other resources, looking for materials to help me set up a worthwhile program.

My first week was a trying situation, one in which I was nervous but made attempts not to show it. I was the lone Black teacher at the junior high. I was the only dark face present, but the majority of the teachers were exceptionally nice. Being a Negro, we have always been sensitive to any adverse surroundings and especially sensitive to any resentment shown towards us by members of other races. It is an instinct that, in my day, could be compared to sixth sense or animal instinct.

That day, as I walked into a sea of White faces, I hid my nervousness deep within. How vividly I remember my first faculty meeting. Little did I dream that I would be the only black on the faculty at

Junior High for the next twelve years. Pre-faculty meetings were always held prior to the formal opening of the school. During this time, specific assignments are given out, and expectations, programming, introductions, etc., are also made. Mr. Lawrence, my principal introduced me, made a pep talk, and had his secretary Irene, begin to pass out folders for home room. I like to think of him as the wonderful grand- old man, for in his way, he tried very hard to make integration work. Although some teachers made attempts to be overly friendly, one could still feel the hostility, the animosity, and stillness which existed in the air. Some of the staff exhibited coolness and disdain. (Being born into a segregated world, it is very easy for one to detect feelings of the White race, no matter how well the attempt to camouflage them may be). This was always felt through a carelessly disguised remark, a small cackle of laughter, or just generally "red-faced expressions" whenever near. They always expressed doubt that we were capable of being superior or as more educated than many of them. Nevertheless, I braved the orientation ordeal with a pasted smile on my face, but deep down within, a fear of some unknown expectation gripped my very soul.

Memories of that very first day are still fresh in my mind. It was a very hot September day. That day, when we greeted the students or (the students greeted me) stands out vividly in my mind, like yesterday. I am sure the children were more curious than nervous, simply because most had never been exposed directly to a Black face and, most of all, to a Negro teacher. Everyone assembled in the gymnasium for a formal opening. Each teacher read off the names of his or her home-room pupils, and they, in turn, followed the teacher into the assigned classroom. My heart went pitter-patter, and perspiration flowed freely under my arms, yet I managed to camouflage my innermost feelings of ambivalence. My feelings were mixed with a bit of joy, a bit of sadness, a bit of irresolution within, and a bit of inner peace without. Yet, I knew and recognized that this was a new day, a new beginning, and a new challenge for me. As I called out each name, a new learning experience came forth, for most names were of German, Czech, or Spanish origin, with relatively few Blacks in the group.

As we marched out of the gym and down the stairs to the basement, we made it to my room. The room was on the first floor or basement of a three-story building. On the second floor was the office, teacher's lounge, principal's office, and classrooms. The third floor was the location of the library and more classrooms. My new assigned room was large and dark and had black window shades on all of the windows to shut out *any* light filtering through. The brick walls were also painted black. It was the size of two classrooms. It had previously been the former Home Economics department and had been converted into a dark room for showing motion pictures. There was no air conditioner. The only air you received was when you raised the windows.

There, over the brick entrance door, were written the words "The Black Room" because the room had once served the purpose of showing all films in the school. *Now*, it was reserved for me - *a Black Teacher*. Thus began my *"Seventeen Years in the Black Room."*

As I stood by the door, greeting my students and inviting them into the room, one of the young men named Joe glanced at the title over the door, looked back at me, and with a smirk said, "Well, that's about right, the *black room*." I think he wanted to illicit a laugh from his fellow classmates and put me in my place or test me on day one, but I just looked at him. I guess after so many years of swallowing pride and ignoring uncouth remarks, I instinctively "pretended" not to hear. His words did not move me to react, but to this day, they stood out in my memory. I resolved then and there that I would survive! I will become a conqueror! I will overcome!

Yes, I heard him, but in my many years of teaching, I somehow learned how to "grin and bear" many things; "hear and don't hear." Still smiling and nervously perspiring, I greeted the class of about 25 or 30 boys. *All* were slow learners or needing assistance with their assignments. I had been assigned five class periods consisting of four classes of all handpicked boys and one class containing six girls. The only brilliant group was the class of six girls. The rest ranged from practically all slow learners and incorrigibles to one or two average learners. The class was predominantly White boys. It was quite obvious that these students were hand-picked for me. Not only were they slow learners, but were also the problem students at the school. So here I was, faced with a double task: teaching them to learn and dealing with disciplinary issues.

My silent thought was, *"What an assignment!"* After having taught grades two through eight high school subjects such as chemistry, shorthand, typing, economics, and history, *I* was relegated to a group of slow primarily White boys. But I accepted this, for to me, it was a challenge. Not a challenge as to my teaching ability, for I felt confident in this, but a challenge to me to test my ability to cope with the situation at hand. This also said to me that the "Supervised Study," in reality, was not supervising study but a way to try and break me. I stood fast and determined that I would not break.

One of my next encounters was with "Tom". He had been labeled as incorrigible and had been a problem child since the first grade. The word was passed from one grade to the next that Tom would spend most of his time in the office. Teachers commented that he would be my headache. When I met him, he did start out as being my problem child as well. However, I had always been able to handle my problems without the office confrontations. So, we began our journey. Each time Tom acted up, I kept him for a few minutes after class, and had him to sign and date his offense. Then, I sent him on to the next class. He proceeded to report me to his mother.

Having known racial prejudice firsthand, I was apprehensive about whether or not the students would accept me. I set out to do what I did best: TEACH! It spoke to the old myth saying to me that "all Black teachers are inefficient and poorly trained," was still in existence. Thus, I realized that this was yet a third challenge, a challenge to disassociate and destroy the myth. Mrs. Jones, the counselor, met with me after school. She said, "Susie, you are to try to bring these children up to their grade levels by the end of the year. They don't know how to study, and some of them are discipline problems. Do you think you can handle it?" My answer was a simple, "Yes. I am sure I can". My inner resolution was, "Try me."

What surprised me was that most of the students did accept me fairly quickly, and I enjoyed working with them.

Strategy on my part had to be developed in two ways: what to do to help them improve and what to do to cope with their behavior problems. I was like a rabbit in the briar patch. I had to devise my own curriculum, map my own course, and follow the same thereafter. For the sake of learning, I gathered assignments, typed and mimeographed worksheets, used other materials, etc., for busy work. I had purchased a book called "How to Study," which taught many study skills. Each day, I designated a special portion of the classroom period, teaching them varied reading skills and how to allot certain portions of their time for studying and developing good study habits. In between, I sandwiched a bit of their homework, giving individual help to students who needed it most. I would copy pages and have students to study and complete assignments. I always went above and beyond to make sure my students learned. I spent evenings developing lesson plans, identifying projects, and writing out worksheets. I gave homework pretty much every day. My students often said they could hear me walking down the hall. When I did, the class often dropped into silence. Sometimes, I worked with three subjects at one time. I found myself teaching history, English, math, and reading, and often, as I look back, I don't know how I did it all.

Progress was being made, but there was still a lot to be gained. The six little girls that I had in my homeroom were average students, so there was a limited amount of supervised study that I had to give them. With permission from the head counselor, I began counseling them on teenage manners, etiquette, and things of this nature, stressing values, the feeling of worthiness, the importance of being somebody, good attitudes, and behavior. This won them over. For within the group, there were two or three diehards who had always been taught that Whites were superior to Blacks. Eventually, there was participation and great enjoyment in this class. So, to me, the Black curtain had been raised just a little more.

The first week I was at Rockdale Junior High, the boys and girls were kept separate and required to be on opposite sides of the building at recess. Black boys and Black girls stayed in their respective groups on each side of the building, as did the White boys and girls. Initially, there was little interaction between the races. It was especially forbidden for the Black boys to be on the girls' side or talking to White girls. This definitely earned a visit to the principal's office.

There were always students who chose to give me a trying time, and at the beginning, discipline problems were prevalent. My principal said to me, "You don't have to take any unnecessary rudeness or other discipline problems. Just send them to me." As I had always been a teacher who could handle her own problems, I still had the confidence in this new situation that I could do the same. I began to gather my options. From the discipline standpoint, I typed and mimeographed behavior expectations, stressing the importance of good manners and good behavior to future life as an adult. I talked to students one-on-one for corrections. I also wrote students up and put their information in my file for future reference if problems continued. The boys were always causing some sort of problem.

Sometimes, but not often, I turned to this last resort - the paddle. It always seemed to work. Being from the old school of teaching, we could use the "board of education" as long as we had a witness. Before I resorted to my "board of education," I quoted my expectations and rules. I only paddled as a last-needed apparatus. A few times, I escorted students to the office for a paddling with Mr. Lawrence, the principal. For those who do not know, there was a time when teachers were able to paddle students who misbehaved. Misbehavior was met with an office visit, the paddle, a call to their parents, and for most Black students and some Whites, another paddling when you got home.

I had the Randy's, the David's, the Lou Ann's, and some of every kind who chose to be talkative and disrespectful and those who refused to try. I talked kindly to each student, pointing out to them the results of disobedience and the obstructions that they could encounter later in life. When that did not work, I used three-by-five cards, wrote up the discipline problem, and had them to sign it so that if it became necessary, I could show the information to their parents. Last, I paddled to the enjoyment of the students. This worked! I even had students to make me a paddle called "Old Faithful," and to this date, it is a part of my memoirs. My "board of education," or paddle, became a decorative object on display in my room, and I seldom sent anyone to the office to be disciplined.

My rules were simple. I wrote maxims on the blackboard, my favorite being, "The only way to be respected is to respect yourself." At the same time, I would take time to explain the maxims to the students. These later became my blackboard rules.

Otherwise, I have the Five R's that were rules for the classroom and behavior: "Reading, Riting, Rithmetic, Respect, and Responsibility. These were carryovers from my 23 years at Aycock. I really never had discipline problems while teaching there.

"If you are to make it in life, you must learn how to read, write, and figure efficiently so that you can carry out your business affairs when you become an adult. If you respect yourself, you can very easily respect others. All I ask of you is that you give me your best respect. It is your responsibility to do your work if you want to succeed. I can't make you do. It is your decision and your priority to want to do."

It was the responsibility of the students to master the 5 R's. My request was that they give me the best respect in the classroom and accept responsibility for giving me their best performance.

As the year rolled on, I became more involved with my work. The sun slowly filtered into the cracks of the "Black Room," illuminating its rays and gently touching the souls of the human occupants. Its warmth penetrated into the dark corners of the minds of the living beings and stamped out some of the prejudicial thoughts that existed. Students settled into the daily learning environment, and incidents became less frequent. I began to see the acceptance by the students of a Black teacher. I began to note a change in overall attitudes. I also began to note improvement in grades for at my request and interest; each student brought me their report cards for review.

It was still apparent that most were not comfortable with the Black students at the Junior High. The punishments for Blacks were often stricter as well. Black students who got into trouble were sent home for three days. As I mentioned earlier, because of the Rockdale zoning laws, it excluded Blacks from riding the bus to school as most Blacks lived across the tracks less than two miles to the school. In order to ride the bus, you had to live more than two miles away. As a result, Blacks either had to have a ride or walk to school. One day, Jay Mason was sent home for a minor incident. Somehow, on his way, as he was crossing the tracks, he was hit by a train. His death was one of a number of train incidents in Rockdale.

My twenty-five boys and six girls mellowed. They began to be very cooperative and worked hard to accomplish something worthwhile. You could just see the progress they were making! By the end of the first semester, my "supposedly low achievers" were making better grades than students who had been categorized in groups according to their scholastic ability. And my having to discipline them was minimal. In fact, I had developed a relationship with the students whereby I could stand quiet outside the door and talk with him or her about their actions and somehow get them to act or behave in a desirable manner. I also kept behavior records with the students' signatures to signify that their behavior was inappropriate, and they acknowledged their actions.

The other teachers began to wonder, 'How do you handle those kids? I always had problems with Frank, Jim, etc.'. My answer to this is simple. "It's all in caring… It's all in being tactful or saying the right thing at the right time. Students need to know that you are interested in their welfare." Day by day, I continued to press forward, working and trying to reach the students, overcoming the obstacles that had been put in my path.

The year rocked on. It was nearing the Christmas holidays. An added responsibility was to assist with the annual Christmas pageant, a highlight in the junior high school. The school's Christmas program was a big thing in Rockdale. The Christmas pageant was an annual tradition and a memorable moment to all students and the community. It was the portrayal of the birth of Jesus Christ. It seems that the entire town looked forward to this occasion.

Each teacher was given assignments or segments of the pageant to train and coordinate. In the old school, I had 23 years of musical experience but was only given the option of helping to select 8th-grade girls who would be the candle bearers and sing 'Star of the East.' I dutifully helped train the girls to sing, but there was a disappointment, for I felt that with my ability and music knowledge, I should have been given more to do. Instead, a White lady with limited experience was given the responsibility for the overall project. She was only with the school for one year and then moved on to new fields.

Each year, at least 150 students participated in this production. Students had to audition for their roles. Mary and Joseph were usually portrayed by the 8th graders. The angels were from grade 6. The pianist, soloist, quartet, and narrators were chosen from those who auditioned. All students had the opportunity to try out, but mostly Blacks were relegated to the huge choir. The general choir was from the entire school. Initially, the Christmas pageant was primarily segregated, like many other things. Only Blacks in the 6th grade could participate in the general choir, and no Blacks had a leading role in the play until some years later. Initially, the quartet, solo, and acting positions consisted of primarily White students.

After a few years, a few Blacks were chosen for the octet and candle bearer positions. Later, Blacks were finally chosen for solos and pianists. Doris P. was one of the early singers in the octet. William was the first pianist for the pageant, followed in later years by Tamara, my granddaughter, for several years. In the solo position, Tommye C. and later my grandson Jerome sang "O Holy Night". Charles C. was cast as the Angel Gabriel one year. Generally speaking, over most years, all main characters were relegated to Whites.

This experience was enjoyable, for it seemed as if students were gradually "mellowing" towards having a Black teacher on the faculty. It was a beautiful pageant, and all of the students played their parts with excellence. The pageant was a success, and after carefully thinking things through, I realized that this was a new step. I was taking another new beginning. Ultimately, all of this went smoothly until the pageant was disbanded decades later.

Meanwhile, all of my fellow Aycock teachers were doing their best to navigate the new waters as well. Because we were all split up at the school, we rarely got a chance to see each other and compare notes. When we did talk, it seemed that there were always eyes on us. Fear of "Blacks" congregating. Many times, we would visit each other's houses after hours to discuss how we were doing, talk about the challenges, and sometimes encourage each other through the next days. I would sometimes stop by Ms. Artie's to talk for a while or Ms. Petty's.

Each year, there was a Rockdale teachers' faculty Christmas party. The 1965 faculty Christmas party "took the cake." We were all reluctantly invited, it seemed, but Black men were not allowed. The school superintendent, Mr. Moorman, said that Laura could attend, but her husband would not be allowed to attend like other faculty members' spouses. Principal Tom Underwood was the message bearer. In response, Laura relayed her message, saying, "If other spouses are invited and can attend, and my husband is the only one excluded, I will not attend." In our own ways, we each took a stance to cement our presence and draw our lines in the sand.

My first Christmas at the junior high brought me a pleasant surprise. One student whose father was a glass blower came to school and presented me with a beautiful hand-blown glass jar, unique in shape. Her father sent it along with a note that I still cherish today. He said that I had paid his child more attention than she had ever received from a teacher, and he really appreciated the work I did with her.

This warmed my heart and just gave me a small ray of hope that I was getting through in some small way. The semester has ended, and the results are in. There was amazement and improvement of the students I had. There was also a bit of wonderment, for it was often mentioned how you can take all of those various subjects and do what you've done with those students.

My philosophy has always been that you must first lend to the confidence of the students. All children need a sense of belonging and true feelings. All children need to know that within themselves, they are important. They are somebody.

My second philosophy, which I've instilled in students throughout the years, is believe in yourself. With this belief, you can accomplish the impossible. The Black curtain continued to rise a bit more, and the light was slowly filtering in.

I called these years from 1954 to 1970 the T years. They were tough and unpredictable. Within that period, there was turmoil, turbulence of war, tragedy, and trouble throughout the land.

CHAPTER 11

Susie's Blackboard

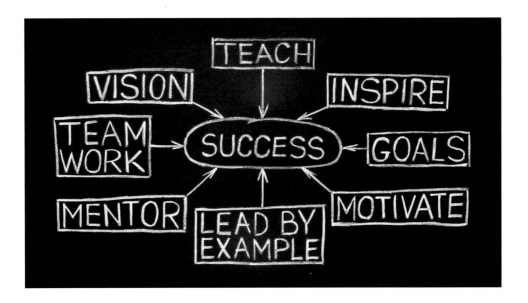

While teaching at Aycock, I rarely, if ever, had to deal with discipline problems. We taught moral principles as well as subject matter, and oft times, we were the only mothers and fathers for some of the children. Unequivocally, we had some of the greatest students who made their mark on society in many positive and impactful ways.

Early in my career, even before integration, I earned the name of one of the meanest teachers around. I was the teacher who did not allow nonsense. The teacher who gave loads of homework, and the teacher who would not let you fail. I was a dedicated teacher who believed that every child had the inward potential to pass. Whenever a special education student was placed in my class, I would always devise a way to make the subject interesting enough so that they could do something to pass the work, and at the same time feel that they belonged.

To manage the classroom, I kept structure and set expectations. Each year I began with my expectations lecture. Throughout my 41 years of teaching in the Rockdale Public Schools, I wrote a maxim or "words of the week" on the blackboard. It would remain at the top of the blackboard for a week.

My motive was to encourage students to do their very best in subject matter, character, and behavior. After the integration of schools, the former Aycock Students had a special reunion, and they honored me, placing many of my maxims on the program. They called me the Blackboard Lady! Little did I realize as I was doing this, many of my sayings would follow me well into retirement. Some are my individual quotes, and some are from collections or quotes that were made by others.

Some of the quotes were my inventions, while others were from various sources. Among these were:

- Success is not measured by numbers nor counted by dollars and cents, but it comes from determination and perseverance.
- Satan uses the past to keep us depressed and the future to keep us worried.
- If we think negative all of the time, we soon become a negative person.
- Believe in Yourself
- Have Confidence that you can achieve. Believe that you can learn, and you will.
- **Don't judge a book by its cover.** Read the contents and search therein.
- **Anger is like a wild horse.** If it is not broken "in," it becomes dangerous.
- **A bully is a coward.** A bully is also like a coral snake. He's beautiful to observe but may strike with deadly force.
- Worry will not solve your problems, but it will change your facial expressions and the color of your hair.
- You cannot successfully expect a good performance from a Cadillac automobile that has the motor of a Pinto in it.
- **It's a Poor Dog That Won't Wag Its Own Tail** - You have to be confident and share your outstanding accomplishments sometimes. Let others know your contributions.
- **Nothing From Nothing Leaves Nothing** - If you do nothing, don't expect a passing grade on your report card, and if you do nothing, you cannot expect to reap rewards.
- **Root Hog or Die Poor Pig-** Common American catchphrase dating from well before 1834, coming from the early colonial practice of turning pigs loose in the woods to fend for themselves, idiomatic expression for self-reliance.
- The beauty of an individual is not what you see on the outside. But the beauty of an individual is what lies within his inner soul and the end results that he portrays.
- **When You Stop… You drop! -** keep working and providing a contribution to society as long as you can. When you give up and quit moving forward, you die.
- Not How Did I Live, But What Did I Give
- Greatness is not found in size, nor height, or depth, but greatness is found in the minds of those who choose to pursue it, capture its resonance, and see it for the benefit of others.
- No matter how educated you may be…. if you fail to respect your elders, you show your ignorance.
- Hatred is like a cancer. If not treated with God's medicine, it will soon destroy your soul.
- Don't let old age be the winter of your life. Instead, think of it as the harvest.

. . .

One day, I learned a lesson from a little plant. Lessons are in the slightest things if we only look for them.

A Lesson From A Little Cacti

'Twas in the early spring when birds began to sing happily as they searched for materials to build new homes. Trees were putting on their green foliage, and farmers were readying the soil to plant their early crops. Plants that had been removed from their sheltered places that served as protection from the cold wintry months had been placed in their summer abodes. One would assume that winter was over and spring had arrived.

But suddenly, Jack Frost, with his beautiful shiny white coat, paid an unexpected visitation, and many of the plants that had been placed in their summer positions suffered from his bite. Being a potted plant lover but never really having a major success, I was somewhat discouraged because my little cacti was among those plants that Jack Frost had chosen. This plant was special because it was a gift from a dear friend. It was green with little white spines, but in its hidden beauty, it managed to camouflage itself, for you could pick it up with your naked hand and not get stuck.

The secret was that "outwardly, it portrayed an appearance of toughness," but "inwardly, there was a tender touch," a special softness and seemingly kindness.

The little cacti grew and grew, and soon, its green nodules had spread all over the pot, making an unusual, beautiful bouquet with its tiny white spines. Not being aware of an oncoming, sudden change of weather, to my surprise, the little cacti suffered tremendous damage. It had dropped its tiny nodules, taken on a burnt brownish color, and withered down to the edge of the pot. It looked so sad and forlorn until I was tempted to "trash" it, but because it was a gift, I relied on my instinct, hoping that watering and perhaps a good rain would revive this plant.

The little cacti seemed to say, "I'm not giving up. I'm going to keep trying." Though unseen, its little roots pushed deeper into the soil to gather the hidden nutrients that had been stored during the winter months.

Six weeks passed swiftly by, and just looking at that little plant gave me an instant feeling that it would never be the same again. In its quiet moments of growth, the little cacti kept saying, "But I'm going to keep on trying."

One bright, shiny morning, I had gone outside to retrieve my daily newspaper, and oddly, it had fallen against the little cacti pot. At a glance, I could see three or four little spiny nodules pushing through the soil and seemingly saying, "I told you I could make it." In a few short weeks, the pot was once again full of harmless, little green spiny cacti nodules. A lesson of life was suddenly revealed to me. "Even though things may seem hopeless at times, if we have faith in God, we can overcome, for with Him, nothing is impossible.

Four lessons learned!

1. Don't always take for granted the things that you see for the first time because often outward appearances are used to protect and camouflage from danger.
2. The inward look is important, for there may be an entirely different personality to view as you become more familiar with surroundings.
3. Nothing is obtained without effort.
4. Don't give up too easily. "If at first you don't succeed, try, try, again!

Each day brings a new dawning, the meaning of new beginnings in the little cacti that continues to live on.

CHAPTER 12

Miseducation

The term "nigger" has taken on pejorative qualities, as it implies not only darkness of skin, but a general lack of intelligence and sophistication and contempt. At the time of the word's origin, various English-speaking North American settlers who set cultural standards considered Black people fundamentally inferior and less civilized than White people.

Negro; *noun*

(pl. **Negroes**) (old-fashioned, often offensive)

1. A member of a race of people with dark skin who originally came from Africa.
From The American Heritage® Dictionary of the English Language, 5th Edition.
1. Noun. Used as a disparaging term for a Black person.
2. Noun. Used as a disparaging term for a member of any dark-skinned people.
3. Noun. Used as a disparaging term for a member of any socially, economically, or politically deprived group of people.

...

Over the years, I remember a select few of my students that were prejudiced. It was evident in their actions and words. I remember Jimmy, one of Rockdale's elites. One day, we were reading a topic in the textbook which contained quite a bit of information about Negroes. He began to read, and each time that he came across the word "Negro", he would politely pronounce "Nigger;" "and the Niggers did such and such," he read. It didn't intimidate me, but it did bring giggles from some of the class. Other students in the class would look at me quizzically. I patiently allowed him to finish reading and went on with my class as usual. At the end of the class period, I required Jimmy to remain after class. I then told him to look up the definition of "Nigger" and then write the correct word, Negro, 100 times. I then required him to carry the paper home and get it signed by his parents. They signed it, along with a note of apology. I never had any more trouble out of Jimmy. In the past, when students did something wrong, part of their punishment may be to write the offense over and over. In this case, correcting the word Negro. In other cases, it might be to write, "I will not use foul language in class or I will not talk in class" 100 times.

Nigger	
Nigger	
Nigger	
Nigger	
Negroes Negroes Negroes	
Negroes Negroes Negroes	
Negroes Negroes Negroes	
Negroes Negroes Negroes	

"Dear L.R.

I had thought of sending this to your mother, but decided that you just don't know any better. Anyone can be called a "nigger" for it is an unbecoming way of acting. As you go through life, remember this: for racial slurs can hurt you and your future, so think about this. Don't use overtones against anyone, regardless of race, creed, or color.

Love,

S. Piper"

"He knows better than this, and I don't believe it will happen again…

Signed: D. MCQ"

• • •

The struggle was still to educate others about the lives and accomplishments of black people. The fight for civil rights continued in and out of the school system. While we quietly went about our business working to prove ourselves in the new territory of integrated education, privately, it was stressful and also gave me a greater sense of accomplishment as I began to reach some students.

Although many came to accept the integration of schools, there were still many things that were separate and many people that insisted on using derogatory terms to describe a people they cared not to understand. The plight of blacks both past and present was reflected in a song that was recognized by blacks as the Negro National Anthem. In 1899, James Weldon Johnson penned a poem to describe the plight of slavery and the glimmers of hope and fortitude held by African Americans. In early 1900, his brother, John Rosamond Johnson, set the poem to music.It began to be sung in segregated schools across the nation in the early 1900's.

The Johnsons were natives of Jacksonville, Florida. James, two years older than John, gained a college education, taught school in rural Georgia and in Jacksonville, and became one of the South's first African American recipients of a law degree. Rosamond received training at musical conservatories in Boston and London, but also returned to Jacksonville to teach. Both men workedat their alma mater, the Stanton School, Duval County's segregated black high school.

Early black migrants to Harlem, James and Rosamond Johnson were respected leaders of the postwar renaissance. James served as general secretary of the New York NAACP and became an outspoken figure for civil rights and against lynching. The song took on new meanings as black migrants spread across the nation and extended campaigns for equal rights. This resilience and determination was reflected in our every day lives to present ourselves as upstanding citizens, to maintain family values, and to exhibit the standard of excellence that we lived by even as we were subjected to differences in assignments, given remedial students, and subjected to lower standards like the Black Room. Head held high, I continued to walk the halls of the Rockdale Junior High with purpose and passion. Treating all of my students with respect and educating them beyond the classroom was my goal.

Lift Ev'ry Voice and Sing- Negro Anthem

By James Weldo Johnson and J. Rosamund Johnson

Lift ev'ry voice and sing
Till earth and heaven ring
Ring with the harmonies of Liberty.
Let our rejoicing rise,
High as the list'ning skies, let it resound loud as the rolling sea.

Sing a song full of faith that the dark past has taught us.
Sing a song full of the hope that the present has brought us.
Facing the rising sun of our new day begun
Let us march on till victory is won.

Stony the road we trod,
Bitter the chast'ning rod
Felt in the day that hope unborn had died.
Yet with a steady beat,
Have not our weary feet
Come to the place on which our fathers sighed?

We have come over a way that with tears has been watered.
We have come, treading our path through the blood of the slaughtered
Out from the gloomy past,
Till now we stand at last
Where the white gleam of our star is cast.

God of our weary years,
God of our silent tears,
Thou who has brought us thus far on the way
Thou who has by thy might,
Led us into the light
Keep us forever in the path, we pray.

Lest our feet stray from the places, our God, where we met Thee,
Lest our hearts, drunk with the wine of the world, we forget Thee;
Shadowed beneath Thy hand,

May we forever stand,
True to our God,
True to our native land.

Miseducation of people happens in all races. The prejudicial statements, racist remarks, and down-the-nose looks signaling your unwanted presence was evident in more than a few people. Whenever I ran into those few, whether student or teacher, I sought the best way to re-educate and, at the very least, address the issue in a tactful way.

For the most part, my relationship with the teachers was good. In most aspects, days were uneventful, and everyone went about their business. It seemed that most of the *male* teachers were friendlier than some of the *females*. Those who didn't care to form a relationship never took the time to speak nor talk. If they saw me coming, they might just walk the other way to keep from speaking. I simply ignored them as well. Some who did attempt to form a relationship were often a farce, for many times, an intentional slip of the tongue in speaking or talking of the Negro children, referred to as the "Nigra" children, let me know exactly what kind of mindset one had. I overlooked this for a *while* until it became obvious that the mispronunciation was intentional. Use of these words sometimes riled the Black students who were trying diligently to fit into their new environments.

Within the school, there were other Black Rooms, whose windows were not covered with black curtains, and whose sign did not read "The Black Room," but whose sign was camouflaged by another sign… *The Faculty Lounge*. This setting became another proving ground. One thing that did get under my skin would happen often in the lounge. The 7th and 8th grade history teachers and I had the same conference period. This was usually around 11 a.m. in the morning. Each day during this time, teachers who were free met there. The three of us would sit in the lounge, sometimes eating, chatting, or working on our lesson plans.

Being quiet in nature, I frequented the lounge but seldom had very much to say. I sat listening to comments, ethnic jokes, etc. until I could no longer take it. One teacher, in particular, the American history Teacher, Ms. V, was constantly referring to the "poor little nigra children." She also had a bad habit of saying "boy" or "girl" to Blacks. I never heard the Texas history teacher, "Dot," say anything derogatory about the black students, but every day, Ms. V had something to say. Many of the students had had an encounter with this teacher, and many were sent home because of "impudence" towards her over this word. Every day, she would walk into the lounge and remark, "The poor little nigger children, they just can't learn," or "I feel so sorry for the poor little nigra children," or "Those little nigra children just can't seem to catch on" or "Those little nigra children have bad attitudes, or they always like to fight." I didn't mind so much of what she said, but the way she would say "nigra".

She kept it up day after day until finally, one day, after a barrage of the word, I said to her, "We pronounce the word N-E-G-R-O"! According to the dictionary, the word "nigra (nigger)" means a way of acting. I voiced my sentiment in a quiet, stern yet very tactful manner, handing her the dictionary and asking her to read aloud the word "nigger". "Anyone could be a nigger." It's not a color or race. I said to her that if she is referring to the children, the correct pronunciation of the word was **NEGRO.** I did not want to hear her use that word again. And besides, I had heard around the community that someone better warn her as there were a few older kids who were plotting and planning to way-lay and hurt her if she kept calling them out of their name.

While it's true that these days, some Blacks themselves often use these terms when talking to one another, and unfortunately, today, in urban speaking, rap, and so forth, but it is an undesirable, derogatory word. It is especially meant negatively when coming from another race, and *"To us,"* I said, *"it is as an unacceptable and the same as your being referred to as poor white trash or red-necks"* or as offensive to Spanish people as being called "wet-backs" or "Diego's". "No one desires, nor should anyone be called out of their name or in a derogatory manner or using racist or prejudicial terms." Inwardly, I prayed. As here I was, a Black teacher seated among six or seven White teachers, voicing my opinion, whereas, in previous years, we had always withheld our innermost thoughts. I guess I had just reached the point that I could not stomach it anymore. Afterwards, I never heard the word again, and we became the best of friends, *so to speak.* Another plus for me had been accomplished!

The light finally filtered over the faculty lounge. From that particular time forward, I was accepted. I was sought after for advice. I had made new-found friends instead of enemies. We shared our problems. We can discuss things freely with no animosity. The upstairs Black Room was filled mostly with warmth and love.

Sometimes, fights broke out. There was an 80/20 ratio of Whites to Black students. When talking with some of the students, I found that their difficulties lay within the classroom, for most deeply resented the references to their ethnic background and usage of the word "Nigra". And, after some unpleasant encounters with Black students and discussions of these matters in the principal's office and the teachers' lounge, these terms slowly began to disappear - *at least* from my hearing. At the same time, the problems existed among the White students, but I never voiced them. I noted also that great efforts were made to keep Black students from associating with White students, even on the playgrounds. Groupings were made within the classroom and were labeled Sections A-B. Usually, Sections A-B-C consisted of the brilliant to average children, while Sections D-E were considered slow learners. The majority of the Blacks, poor Whites, and Mexicans were placed in Sections D and E. In sections A, B, or C, there may have been one or two Blacks and one or two Mexicans.

Principal Lawrence called me into the office one day. He said, "Susie, I'm just having so many problems with some of the Black children. I need your help. Can you come up with any ideas that can help our school? You've had counseling and guidance. And I'm sure you have something."

I said, "Mr. Lawrence, give me a few days to think about this, and I'll get back to you." There had been such animosity or much animosity between some of the White teachers and students. The inferences of the word nigger in the classroom, the fights between Blacks and Whites. There were attempts of some of these teachers to maintain segregated playgrounds but integrated athletic programs. Only on the athletic field was there no distinction, for the school relied upon the athletic ability of the Black students. The unfairness of many grading processes and on and on and on. I thought carefully about the situation and made my decision. I felt that maybe with a small input, I would be able to help alleviate many situations that existed. So, I agreed to help.

My first suggestion was that records be kept on all behavior problems and that these records be signed by the student and witnessed by the teacher and principal. I also suggested that the method of punishment be noted. This was a first for the school and a process that was still in place at the time of my retirement. I could see definite change in most of the students. But there also existed some animosity among my own race because I had been called in to assist and advise.

It began to happen that whenever a problem arose with a Black student, I was called in to be a witness to the punishment, chastisement, or discipline to be meted out. It didn't matter where I was or what I was doing. Being a certified counselor also gave me the opportunity to suggest setting up a discipline program. I suggested that a card file containing dates of the offense and a description of the misbehavior be kept. The student had to sign the record. This started the first discipline program at the Rockdale Junior High. The plan worked very proficiently. The only problem I ever really encountered was, unfortunately, from my own people across the tracks.

All of the issues in school didn't come from White people. Some Black parents were also difficult to deal with, especially when you were correcting a problem student. Some felt that now that the schools were integrated, their children would get a better education from White teachers and felt their children shouldn't have to have a Black teacher. Yes, there was prejudice among our race as well. In some cases, some of the Blacks were nastier to people of their own race than others.

One young lady, that I'll call Edna, was accused of stealing a watch from a White girl in P.E. class. It had been proven that she actually took the watch, and she was sent to the office. As *usual*, the principal called me in to witness. Her mother disliked this action tremendously. When it was decided that she stole the object, she was sent home. School had ended for the day, and I had gone home. Mr. Lawrence called me, and he said, "Susie, Mrs. Carver called me up, and she made some threats concerning you. I just want you to know that if she makes any attempt on you to, let me know and I'll have the law to take care of her." I thanked him with the thought in mind that these are my people. Surely, I could talk with them. Well, fortunately, I met Edna's mother at a funeral several days later, and she was most pleasant and polite. In later years, she came to me and was thankful to me for my help. One thing that I'll always remember is that Mr. Lawrence gave his teachers that needed support.

In a few years, Edna dropped out of school and ended up in prison for *what*, I don't know. It was sad, but sometimes, parents who are overly protective of their children and/or don't try to find out the truth can damage them in the long run.

Then, there were other challenges with integration. There were the teachers and students that always wanted to point the finger at Blacks. One teacher, Ms. Fair, always remarked that the young Black boys were flirting with her. These were 7th and 8th grade boys. She was a plain, skinny, White woman. Homely at best. It was laughable and albeit disgusting that she stooped to such a conclusion. She really hated the Black boys and was always looking for a way to get them in trouble. Unfortunately, that was the way of the world and some people.

Looking back over my first year of integration, I find that if you can compete with self, if you can conquer self, and if you can maintain self, your job is 95% complete. The most important lesson learned in my first year was that regardless of race, creed, color, or surrounding circumstances, all children need love, understanding, guidance, and the feeling that there is someone to share their problems with, whether they be small or great. I went through the first year with little major difficulty. Another conquest. Another barrier removed. In many places, there still remains those dark curtains that have been raised a tiny bit to let in the rays of sunlight. My struggle in the Black Room continues, for I must strive to eliminate those Black curtains.

CHAPTER 13

Trauma and Heartache

The next few years or the years between 1967-1970 were like a scene out of a movie. The things that happened were somewhat like "Close Encounters of the Third Kind", strange and at first unbelievable.

My youngest daughter, Eula, had graduated from nursing school, was teaching nursing education, and working at Brackenridge Hospital in Austin. She had married, divorced, and become a single mother of two children. The oldest, Tamara, was called Happy, a name given to her by the Armstrongs, who lived next door to her kindergarten. She was active, brilliant, and precocious. Every day, her job was to place plates, silverware, etc. on the table for meals. In those days, the family all sat at the table and ate together. My oldest daughter was married and living out of state with her husband and two children.

March 15th, 1968, was a joyous weekend, for we spent a special day of worship together. The joy of E.J.'s life was our three-year-old granddaughter, Tamara (Tammy), performing her special task of setting the table for a delicious meal. Sunday afternoon, E.J. returned to Tomball for his job on Monday.

Later that week, I kept Tammy busy setting the table with silverware in preparation for dinner. March 18,1968, at 6:30pm will always stand out in my memory. Happy gathered her four usual four plates, but all of a sudden, she put one back in the cabinet, saying, "I'm not going to put a plate for Paw-Paw. He's not coming back.' I said "oh, you can put his plate there on Friday when he comes in on Friday". She shook her little head emphatically and said "No, Ma-ma. Paw-Paw is not coming back anymore." I never gave a thought to her words, but they would later haunt me. Later that evening, around 9:00 p.m., the phone rang, and I received the news that my husband passed away in his sleep late that afternoon. On March 18, 1968, he returned to the place where he was rooming with his sister, laid down to take a short nap, and died in his sleep. The doctor diagnosed it as Coronary Thrombosis due to excess stress He was only 56- years old at the time.

One cannot imagine what a shocking and devastating experience this was to me. One moment, I was preparing for his arrival home; the next, I am being notified that he was dead. I was just 43 years old and a widow. It was one of the worst times of my life. Shock, confusion, and frustration wracked my body. What would I do? How would I make it alone? I moved through a fog as I prepared to bury my husband. Overnight, I had another transition. This became a time where I had to suddenly pick myself up, so to speak. I had to make arrangements, transport his remains from Tomball, secure funds by a burial plot, and etc. I had to take over the finances, learn about all of the household bills, take over the banking, pay for a funeral, purchase burial plots, headstones, and continue to work.

I found that I had many friends during this difficult time. The funeral home and bank employees helped me to make arrangements. The funeral director said to me, "Don't worry about payment now. You can handle things your way, for we feel that you will somehow pay us." They allowed me to establish accounts and make payments on the burial plots, caskets, and vault. The people at the bank helped me to organize finances, and taught me about investing, allowed me to pay for things with credit, and gave me advice. Much of what I learned about finance, I learned during this time. I gratefully accepted this help and valued the friendships forged during this time throughout my life.

Here I was, adjusting to a new environment, new school, new people, and now my husband, the father of my children, my partner was gone. In my heart, I knew that integration killed him, like a number of other Black men from the community that year. Essentially, the stress of losing a job, being kicked out of the teaching profession, or having to look for another job to support their families caused them to lose their lives. Integration treated those men similar to slavery. In general, slavery had no use for the Black men as head of a family. It didn't matter if they were college-educated or laymen. They were simply chattel to be pushed and pulled, castrated and bred. Black-balled from fear. Pulled away from their homes their families, separating them from their communities their churches and ostracizing them to the few towns where they could find work. The decision to eliminate all Black male teachers in the county in order to keep Black men from teaching the White girls ultimately served to eliminate their ability to make a living in the area. This also happened in many of the surrounding counties. This, in turn, created tremendous stress for the men. It was all too much for the hearts to bear. That year, at least six men that I knew, fellow teachers, husbands, and fathers, died suddenly. Two others passed away the same spring, in the same manner. And I, like many other women, took on the role as head of the family unit.

The shock of E.J.'s death was tremendous, but it seems that at the end of a dark tunnel, there is always a light, and in spite of the tragedies we experience, there is always some good things. The many beautiful cards and letters I received from my students boosted my spirits. My students proved to me that I had won their love and respect. I have never received as many comforting letters and cards as I did during this difficult and confusing time. Many beautiful sentiments and expressions of sympathy, calls, flowers, food, and loving support from the faculty members and my students helped to lift the indescribable burden. I still cherish many of these sentiments dearly. I had grown to love those twenty-three boys, six girls, and others in my homeroom, as well as others with whom I had contact each day wrote me some of the most beautiful and consoling letters I've ever received. The compassion, the love, the humility shown proved to me that everyone counts and that everyone is one of God's little creatures possessed with the same spirit of love and care for mankind.

My entire town and community gave me their support. E.J., in his death, became a celebrated citizen for his service, and his funeral was held at a White church in town. His funeral was the only Black funeral, to my knowledge, that was ever held at one of the White churches during this time. It was held at the Murray Street Church of Christ, and the entire community turned out to provide their condolences.

After E.J.'s death, I stayed away from school for just one week. After returning, just being around the children was a way to cope with my grief. Over the next few months, I worked to pay for E.J.'s burial and keep myself busy. A number of the people around town sought me out to give me kind words and offer help. Although my husband's death was fresh and my heart broken, the first year at school still continued. Reflecting back, I can truthfully say that the kids were my sustaining factor, for I shall never forget how sympathetic they were and how they poured out their hearts in the sweet little letters they wrote to me. I have placed these in a scrapbook, for they are some of my most precious possessions accumulated during my teaching career.

After my loss, *most* of the teachers had warmed up a bit. But whenever we were in the lounge for coffee or snacks, you could still feel that air of animosity mixed with a feeling of superiority from some of them. I shall never forget how Walter, one of the coaches and P.E. teacher, would act if I entered the lounge. He would turn red, refuse to look my way, and in a few minutes, he would leave. This didn't bother me, for I was born in a segregated world, attended and graduated from segregated schools, and so I did not feel intimidated or inferior. I felt within me that I had achieved rapport with my students, and my principal approved, and in due time, I would fit in.

Through my grief, I had to keep putting one foot in front of the other. Weekends were the worst, for it was then that I became a zombie. My neighbors recognized my state of mind and began to invite me to various activities. At home, I struggled to help my daughters, who were now adults, through the grieving process. I also, as an only child, worked to support my parents and two small grandchildren. Meanwhile, I was also a keeper of my two grandchildren (Tamara and Jerome), so this brought some comfort.

Widowhood also had its challenges There are times in life when we smile, and everything goes well. Then there are times in life when we cry, and we hit those bumps in the road, sometimes making it necessary to detour, take a different fork in the road, and rearrange our lives altogether.

I supposed many forks in the road came without warning when I became a 42-year old widow. E.J. was twelve years older than I. I leaned on my community and church family as much as I could, but it was short-lived. There were so many pressing issues that I had to face until I had to come to grips with myself just to think clearly each day, and yet give a good performance in the work world.

A new life and a new adjustment had to be made. It was so strange, because it seemed that because I was a so-called young widow, everyone felt that it was immediately necessary that I needed a man in my life. I had a good marriage, so at the time, I was not interested in searching for a new "companion" right away.

It was so ironic, for two weeks after final rituals, the minister who gave the eulogy came by (supposedly) to see how I was fairing. He knocked on the door, and I invited him in. He said "I came by to see how you are getting along, and if you need anything in particular." I replied: "Thank you for calling. I am doing alright thus far." I was not particular about him remaining any length of time, for I felt that he should be enroute to his home in Austin to see about his wife, who reportedly was ill. He proceeded to the door, and I said, "Have a safe trip home, and give my regards to your wife." He looked at me, and suddenly decided to try to embrace and kiss me. I have always been courteous to people, but being caught in this position, suddenly I angrily said "If you know what is best for you, go home to your wife, and don't bother coming by to see about me anymore." This was only my first fork in the road, and I was greatly disappointed, because my confidence and trust had been invaded.

Perhaps two or three weeks had passed. My sister-in-law and her husband were in Rockdale each Sunday, for he was a minister to the church that our family attended. This Sunday, they brought a gentleman from McGregor to visit the church. After service ended, they came by to see me, bringing this friend. Poor, poor, dumb me! I thought they were stopping to offer assistance, when suddenly my sister-in-law said "We brought Mr. Albertson to church with us, and we would like for you to meet him. Perhaps you can chat or have dinner together sometimes." My mind began to race. I was saying on the inside 'That's your brother, we just buried! How dare you! And you are bringing someone by to see me?' But kindhearted me said, "Thank you. I appreciate your interest in my welfare." I am sure the expression on my face let them know that I did not appreciate their match-making motives.

From time to time, I was pestered by various men, but still living under a cloud of shock and grief, I had absolutely no interest in anyone. To top it all, another shock came from a member of the church. One of the church elders called my home. He was a well-groomed (gentleman), always dressed to the nines, owned a nice car, making plenty of money; but was not attractive to me at all. He felt that he was "God's special gift to all women", and that any woman he chose to chase would soon be his paramour. He also had a wife, but this didn't matter to him. He proceeded to tell me how pretty I was and said he planned to come to my house and have his way with me. I was shocked that an upstanding church member would behave this way.

He began calling me, and if I happened to go to a store in town, he would trail in behind me trying to talk to me. If I stopped at the gas station to purchase gasoline, some how he would pop up on his special motorcycle. He would say, "You are such a nice lady. You need a real man to take care of you. I would be so nice to you. I would just do things for you beyond your imagination." His words just seemed to churn my stomach. I tried to be nice, but it was becoming more difficult, for I felt as if I were being stalked. A feeling of hatred began to infest my well-being.

I would hurriedly get out of the store, or hang up the telephone, saying "Don't call me. I am not interested in you. Besides, you have a wife and daughter that you should be seeing about." This feeling of dread and spirit of hatred seemed to become like a disease that kept spreading into the venues of my mind. This wasn't me, for I have never disliked or hated anyone.

Being nice did not help. Every night around 11:00 p.m., those persistent calls came. Too bad, we did not have caller I.D. in those days. He was determined, insistent, and somewhat insolent, making mild threats to invade my privacy.

I told my daughter what was happening, and she bought me a pistol. It had a pearl handle. The calls continued. He called again. "If you don't let me come to your house, I will come anyway when I get ready, and I will just break your door in." Another threat, I said to myself. In those days, you only had a little door latch on your screen door, and you used a skeleton key for the main door.

Murderous thoughts were becoming an obsession, yet I did not want to disgrace my reputation, nor my immediate family, and I knew that reporting harassment to the police would be in vain. The next time he called with those threatening words, I calmly told him: "You are very welcome to come to my home, if you so desire, but when you put your foot on the first step, I am going to leave you lying there." Why hadn't I thought of this before? The phone calls stopped.

I was glad I made this threat, for I know I would have become a murderess, and would have to live with this cruel deed for the rest of my life. Those happenings caused me to leave the church where my family and I worshipped, for I had become disgusted with my so-called Christian brothers, and they had touted themselves as spotless members in a spotless church.

I started to feel even more alone as the married women gravitated away from me. I suspected, that some of the separation I felt was for two reasons: first, from fear because I was now part of a new club - the widowers club. It was almost as if other ladies were afraid, it was something they could catch. Second, as I indicated, I was still fairly young and attractive - the second reason was jealousy, although

I had no remote desire for anyone else's husband. This was all just too much. I lost respect for those men, the elders who had served the church with my husband. It was time for me to find a new church home. After that, I left the church my husband and I attended and started to make plans for yet another transition. My life changed greatly, and I managed to overcome and find some happiness; but, I have often wondered what would have happened to me, if I had not taken a special fork in the road.

Summer 1968 at 6:30 a.m., I had all but dismissed Happy's statement about E.J's death until another incident arose. Happy got out of bed, runs in the kitchen and says "Ma-Ma, Mr. McGregor got his throat cut last night down in the flat. He didn't die, but they had to take him to the hospital. I politely shooed It off saying, "you just had a bad dream. You don't even know Mr. McGregor, and you probably just heard someone call his name some time." Oddly though, she had not been outside. There were no grown-ups in the house to have brought up the McGregor name. So, another idea was dismissed.

At 1pm, I ventured out into my year. My neighbor said, "Did you hear the news?" I said, "What news? I haven't talked to anyone." Then she said Happy's exact words. "Mr. McGregor got his throat cut last night at Ruby's place. They had to take him to the hospital but he's ok." This was my second encounter of the third kind. I began to take notice of little things Happy said, and at the same time began to wonder if God had given her the gift of extra sensory perception or E.S.P.

The years 1968-1969 brought more new changes. I was *still* the only Black teacher on the faculty, but by this time, I had become accustomed to this. I had a new assignment of teaching two 7th-grade reading classes. This showed increased confidence in my teaching ability. I still had the same assignments outside of the classroom duties, with the exception that I was now to accompany the new junior high choir with the band man directing. We made a great success of this choir, performing some songs such as *Jesus Christ Superstar*, which was a very popular song at this time. Unfortunately, the choir was discontinued some years later.

At the end of the year, "Dot," the Texas history teacher retired, and also Ms. V, the American history teacher. Most activities and interaction between the children were still segregated by instinct and choice for the most part. The only place that this was less obscure was in sports, as the Black boys were athletic, and the school wanted them to participate for competitive sports. By comparison they were accepting of Black coaches to a certain extent, but they didn't last but one year.

My second year was quite unobstructed. I was assigned to the 7th grade math classes and three supervised study classes. Along with teaching, I had the worst discipline problems within 7th and 8th grades. I was settling into my new role, and the students were becoming more accustomed to my rules and methods. I decided that I must devise some method of punishment other than whipping, etc. So, I started a point system on conduct and grades. This worked nicely, for no one wanted to carry home a poor grade in deportment. I knew in every method, there is some trial and error, but somehow, my plans always worked, and I deeply felt that God was with me all the way.

Then, Mr. Lawrence called me to the office and asked me if I would like to teach 7th-grade history. I accepted and, for the next 15 years, remained in this position.

CHAPTER 14

Life Throws You Lemons and Curve Balls

My second Christmas at Rockdale Junior High, I received a pair of handmade measuring cups from one of my Hispanic student's family. I started to see more positive results from my students. After Christmas had come and gone, we started the new semester.

Shortly after, near Easter, tragedy struck again. Months after my husband's death, Happy's mother, my youngest daughter, had been hired as an instructor at El Centro College of nursing in Dallas, Texas, and was at the time, searching for a safe place to live for her family. Happy and her little brother, Jerome, were living with me during this period. The date was April 4, 1970. I was awakened by my granddaughter in the early morning hours. She was just five years old at the time and her brother was three. Happy went into the bathroom. She stayed so long that I went to see if something was wrong. She began talking. "Ma-ma, Ma-ma, I had a bad dream. Momma Eula is in a car wreck. The car caught fire, and Mama Eula burned up. It's all burned up!" she cried. "I got out, but I don't know what happened to JeMe (as she called her little brother." I pulled her close to me and into my bed, quietening and assuring her that it was just a bad dream. As she settled down and her cries subsided, I lay awake, tears welling in my eyes as I waited. I knew my daughter was enroute home, and I said a prayer for her safety.

The strong knock on the door came at my mother's house about 9:30 a.m. At 9:30 a.m., April 4, 1970, my mother, who lived two blocks away, called me and said, "come to the house right away!" I bundled the babies up and immediately responded. The highway patrolman was awaiting me as I opened the door. He gave me the news of my daughter's sudden death, repeating almost verbatim what Happy told me hours earlier. I screamed. The guttural sound came somewhere from deep within as I sank to the floor. The policeman explained that he was sorry, but my daughter had been killed in a fiery head-on collision between Rose-Bud and Marlin. She had been on her way to Rockdale from Dallas, for the weekend to see her children. She and another nurse collided on a narrow two-lane highway, and her car exploded. The other nurse was in critical condition but lived. There was nothing left of my daughter and her car, so to speak. I cried to go to her, to see for myself, but the patrolman told me that he would fight me before he let me see her. A neighbor and a family member provided the identification. She was so badly burned that I had to make arrangements for a funeral and bury her two days later.

Shock, grief, distress, fear, and sadness invaded my body. There is nothing that can ever compare to the loss of a child, and one never ever gets over it. Even so, I knew that I had to keep going. I had a new family to rear, so this time, I was immediately forced to pick up the pieces. I was designated as guardian for my two little grandchildren (Tamara /Happy and Jerome). This was just two years and two weeks after E.J.'s untimely death. I had just finished paying for his funeral and grave plots ten days ago, and here I was again! Now, not only did I have no husband, but I lost one of my precious daughters *and* was left with two small children (ages 3 and 5) to raise. I wondered why God was giving me so much heartache and grief. How was I going to make it through?

Once again, the children, the community, and now the parents helped me to live through my grief. It was so great that it threatened to overwhelm me, and it was something that I knew I would never recover from. The loss of a child is something from which a mother never gets over. It is a loss so deep, so animalistic, that it seeps into your bones, into your DNA, into the very fabric of your being. Now, I had two little ones to care for.

There comes a time in everyone's life when everything you do seems to bring a measure of heartache and grief. Life just seems to turn upside down, and it often seems as if there is no place to go. But there is always hope. There is always light at the end of the tunnel, and it is up to us to find the hope that will keep us going. My hope, my consolation came from the Divine word of God and especially Psalms 121.

I remember during this time walking through a fog. One day after Eula died, I went into the fabric shop. Tammy, just five at the time, needed to go to the bathroom. I approached the clerk and asked her to let her use the restroom. She said, "No. We don't have a restroom for you." I said, "She is just a little girl; could you please just let her go?" "Take her around the back and let her use the alley," she said nastily. This was in 1970. As if I didn't have enough on my mind, I politely left the store. Needless to say, my business was always taken elsewhere after that day.

The death of my daughter had taken a toll on both my parents, and each one had a stroke within a year of her death. First, my mother, then my father. My mother recovered with only some slight damage, but my father suffered paralysis along his left side and was relegated to a nursing home for care. This added one more task to my day, for I went to the home every day to see my Daddy and make sure he was receiving proper care. I would return home late in the evenings, cut out patterns for clothes I would make for myself and the children, and get ready for the next day. Although many days I buried my feelings and focused on taking care of my family, I kept working to provide the best teaching experience to the children that I could.

My grandchildren and I settled into a working routine. I would get up early to make breakfast and warm the house before waking up my two grandchildren, Tamara and Jerome. I then combed hair - Tammy had a LOT! And off we went to school. The next-door neighbor's grandson rode with us. He and Jerome were a year apart. I would make my way to school for staff meeting and then tackle the classes for the day. After school, we went to Mama's for dinner, to the nursing home to see Daddy, and then home to get homework done. Fortunately, they still lived down the street.

I would pin Vogue and Simplicity patterns and have Tammy cut them out. I made all of our clothes, so I would often sew late at night. Once the children were in bed, always by 10 p.m., I would get ready for bed myself, read the 23rd Psalms or the 121st Psalms, say my prayers, and get ready to repeat the day. And so, I continued day after day. As the children grew up, I added the many extra-curricular activities they participated into my daily routine: band, football games, piano competitions, community plays, and the like. Although it made for a long and tiring day, I was proud and encouraged them to participate wherever they could. Keeping children busy leaves little time for them to get into trouble. My routines were set as I kept my focus on raising my two grandchildren and providing them with the love, foundation, and structure that they needed to survive.

CHAPTER 15

Tamara- Memories of Life with Mama

As I met the challenge of penning my grandmother's aka (Mama's) biography, I faced the realization that there were so many things that Mama endured in her long life that she shielded from my brother and I. My name is Tamara Suzette Hebert Powell, and I am the granddaughter of Susie Sansom-Piper.

As a small child, kindergarten in fact, I remember skipping through the Armstrong's yard, next to the Rocking R kindergarten to cross the street at the old Junior High. The Armstrongs always stood outside as I skipped through their yard and picked up a pocket full of pecans. They would talk to me and watch while I crossed the street to enter the building where Mama taught. Once there, I would walk up the stairs to the second floor. Her room was now the first room on the corner, and she was teaching history. When I got older, I always heard her story about the black room, but I was never in that room. The big kids in her class would look at me and talk to me as I entered and took my seat in the back of the room. I would dutifully read a book or listen to Mama teach until it was time to go home. Sometimes the big kids would smile or joke with me, but Mama maintained order in her classroom so there wasn't much foolishness occurring. I would sometimes see Mama walked down the hall to the office to witness the paddling of a boy spread eagle against the tiled walls. After the bell rang, I could go to the office with her where Mrs. Spears, a pretty lady with dark brown hair, would often give me a piece of candy or ask me about school.

Mama was always smartly dressed and her hair perfectly curled. She made most of her clothes or took patterns to another local seamstress. She was always professional and neat. She especially loved shoes. When she walked to or from the classroom, I could always tell it was her. The click clack of her heels on the green tiles served as a warning to the classroom to be quiet. I noted that her students dared not disobey in her classes. When she walked into a room, everyone immediately became silent and jumped into their chairs if they were out of place. Her commanding presence made her seem like a giant in my eyes. Every day, I made the same path from kindergarten across the street to the old junior high. After school, we headed to get groceries at City Food Market and McVoy's. The McVoy's and Doss's were really nice. Mama would buy fresh meat and vegetables, my favorite summer sausage, and she would always let us have a treat. I would read the comic books in the small magazine area while she shopped. Richie Rich and Archie comics were my favorites. I could spend hours in the book section if allowed. I was an avid reader and had a collection of various paperbacks, Nancy Drew and Hardy Boys at home. I loved going to the store and the Doss's would talk to me from the counter while Mama shopped.

I didn't know anything about integration of the schools. I went to kindergarten with predominately white kids and I didn't much know the difference. I knew we lived across the tracks, but that was just the way life was. I played with everyone and Mama never said anything about people treating us differently. Sometimes at the junior high, I would notice some of the teachers staring or having funny looks on their faces, but I just thought they were mean and old. I steered clear of those teachers. I sat quietly in the back of Mama's classroom, watched, and listened to the goings on. Some of the kids would try to engage me in chatter or play with me when Mama wasn't looking; but, I usually drew or read a book until the school bell rang. After school, Mama would walk to the office to have a brief discussion and I would sometimes go and talk to Ms. Sphere, the secretary. She was nice and was pretty. I remember she had black hair that was sort of teased on top. Mr. Lawrence was nice to me also. Sometimes he gave me candy when I stopped by.

April 1970, my life was different. I didn't know what day it was. I remember being in bed and suddenly I was standing on the side of the road. It was dark. I stood there frozen and watched as two cars collided forcefully head-to-head. A large explosion ensued with a big ball of fire. I could feel the heat on my head and hands. The brilliant orange blaze hurt my eyes and I peered through the fire to see. I saw my mother crumple to the back-seat and I was sure I saw her frantically trying to loosen the seat belt that had been buckled for her safety. I didn't see much of the other car. I just stared through the fire, watching, until it was all over. I awoke crying and in a cold sweat. I was back in my bed, but the vision from the side of the road was fresh in my mind. I could feel the heat from the fire. Still crying I went to Mama Susie's room and woke her. I told her what I had seen, and that Mama Eula was not coming home again. She pulled me into her bed and rubbed my head while I cried, assuring me that it was only a bad dream. Several hours later, my dream became an all too real, reality.

I remember hearing a knock at the door followed by a blood curdling scream. I watched as Mama crumpled to the floor when the highway patrolman delivered the news of my mother's death. I had never heard anything so painful in my life. The scream pierced my soul. I never forgot it. The men would not take Mama Susie to see my mother. They handed her a bag of charred papers, books, and burnt coins. This was all that was left from the car and scene. Mama Susie was told that my mother had been burnt beyond recognition, and that someone else would need to identify her body. The man said he would fight her before he would let her see my child. I thought back to the vision I had and determined I would never wear a seatbelt again. Although, at the time, seatbelts were not a law or necessity. The patrolman did say that my mother was killed instantly and all of her bones were broken. I was never really sure because of my vision. For years to come, I feared wearing a seat-belt and car accidents where I could be trapped.

Two days later, I remember wading through a sea of people. I wore a little purple dress and stood holding my little brother's hand behind a big bronze casket. The old New Hope Church had a balcony, and I watched as people stared at us wading through the large crowd. People lined both sides of the street from beyond my Big Mama's pink house on the corner and down the block to the church. They were hanging over the balcony inside. I remember sitting on the front row, watching the sea of faces looking at me. Some shook their heads. Others cried quietly. Still others stood perfectly still and observed the proceedings. Most looked shocked. To my knowledge, my mother was the first tragic death of a young person during that time. She was 26 years old. Because my mother was burned beyond recognition, there was no time for preparations, no embalming, and no one from the family could see her. Everything happened really quickly.

Later that night, after the funeral, I remember sleeping with Mama Susie. As I lay in the bed, I looked into the open closet door and I saw my mother, Eula. She was wearing a hot pink flowered dress. One that I recognized her wearing often. She hovered in a mist, looking over me before slowly dissipating and disappearing. I woke Mama Susie to show her; but, Mama was gone. I never saw her again. I was left with the fear of fire, gas pilot lights, and open closet doors.

After the funeral, we settled into day- to- day life. Mama Susie never really let us see her sad or grieving; but, often she was quiet and sometimes she stared into space and seemed to be thinking of things far away. Mama took great care of us with the help of Big Mama. I know now just how difficult those years had to be. The other thing is that people in town always said I looked *exactly* like my mother. Everyday, I was a reminder of the baby daughter she lost. While Mama loved me immensely and was proud of me; I often reflect on how difficult it must have been to conceal those feelings from my brother and I, in order to give us a stable home life. Occasionally, we would hear Mama cry; but, she would never tell us what was wrong. She just tried to stay busy and keep us busy doing positive things.

As a young child, I saw her she demonstrate fearlessness and strength to us on a daily basis. Mama was the strongest person I knew. We watched her day in and out, rising before dawn to warm the house with the old gas heaters, before waking us for school. Mama worked hard to take care of Jerome and I. She would wake up early in the morning to make breakfast and comb my hair. I had an awful lot of hair so it took her almost an hour every morning just to comb it. Mama would start breakfast after making sure the house was warm, kneading the dough for her famous angel biscuits and cutting them with a little round biscuit cutter. We would often be served these biscuits with bacon or sausage, rice or oatmeal, and sometimes half of a grapefruit. Mama even bought each of us our own favorite syrup. Jerome loved Brer Rabbit and Delta syrups. I only liked Mrs. Butterworth.

In the evenings, after grocery shopping, we would go to Big Mama's house (Eula Bell), where she would have dinner ready and waiting. Big Mama kept us when we got sick. She cooked the evening meals where she, Mama, Jerome and I would sit around the little table in her kitchen and eat. Mama and Big Mama would talk about the day, the community, and the happenings while my brother and I poked fun at each other and sometimes tried to decipher their code talk. We knew not to interrupt the conversation or interject our thoughts. These were still the days where children didn't interfere in grown peoples' conversations.

On other days, before going home, Mama might stop by to talk with Mrs. Artie or Mrs. Petty. I never knew what they talked about. I just remember squirming in the car during these long conversations and being ready to go home. Now, I realize that these were the only times that they could congregate and compare notes due to the separation at the schools after integration. It's odd how some people get nervous when blacks are together versus other races. Apparently, the separation was by design as the few teachers brought over were all assigned to different schools and grades. Mrs. Petty was in the high school, Mama in the Jr. High, and Mrs. Artie in special ed. Mrs. Battle had special ed but was later assigned to first grade. All separate. They had no staff meetings together and little to no interaction at school. Funny how you learn things later when at the time it all appeared normal. After these occasional visit, we would finish errands and return home.

One day, I remember going to the fabric shop with Mama. I was probably around 5 or 6 and I had to use the restroom really really bad. I asked Mama and she spoke with the lady there; but, the lady told her the bathroom was not for me. I heard Mama say, "she's just a little girl", but the lady still said no. I remember Mama grabbing my hand and walking out of that shop. I don't ever remember going there again.

In the summer, Mama would take us to Mr. Lawrence's farm where we would get to pick dewberries. These were my favorite because Mama would let us eat them with sugar or she would come home and make a dewberry cobbler. Mama also canned peaches, plums, made jelly and jams for us to eat throughout the year.

When I was 7, Mama married a preacher from Elgin. Rev. J.A.Piper. Life became a balancing act as we were constantly transitioning from Rockdale to the Austin area. Church was a regular way of life and each Friday evening after school, Mama would make the drive to Austin where we would attend his church. Saturdays were spent at the church while Mama produced the weekly bulletins, played for the Sunshine kids choir, and rehearsed for Sunday. On Sunday mornings, we would get up early for Sunday school, attend church, and often afternoon service. Some Sundays we spent the afternoon at the home of parishioners for Sunday dinner. Finally, we would pack up and head back to Rockdale to get ready for school the next day. At one point, Mama considered getting a teaching job in Austin; but, a series of events, her parents well-being, as well as her observation of education in the Austin area led her to change her mind. Quite swiftly, she decided to maintain our home in Rockdale and continue to educate us there. Thus continued a thirteen-year journey on the highway between Austin and Rockdale.

In the evenings, once we were home from school, it would be time for me to practice my piano, clean the house, do homework, or other chores. Mama started me in piano lessons when I was five. Mama would often have me cut out sewing patterns. She taught me to follow the lines and pin the pieces to the latest piece of fabric she had purchased. She made all of our clothes (mine and hers). As an expert seamstress, we often spent Saturdays in the fabric shops where she let me pick patterns and material for the next new outfit. Mama would sew late into the night before rolling her curly hair, saying prayers, reading her bible, and retiring for the night to do it all over again.

As I entered elementary and then junior high, routines changed, as Grandpa Bose was now confined to a nursing home. He had suffered a stroke shortly after my Mama Eula was killed in the car accident, and Big Mama could no longer keep him at home. Therefore, every day after school, we would go to the nursing home in Taylor to see Grandpa, before returning home to dinner and evening routines. We always helped to feed Grandpa at dinner time. Mostly, he would really only eat for Jerome. With everyone else, he would clamp his jaws shut and stubbornly refuse to take in the offering. Big Mama drove to Taylor every single day until she could no longer see well enough to be on the road like that. At that time, Grandpa was moved to Rockdale in order to put him closer to home.

When I look back on it now, I see how much Mama did even the simplest things to make us happy. After breakfast, we would head to school. Usually this was in a rush because my brother had a habit of going into the bathroom in the morning and falling asleep again instead of getting dressed. This was a daily consternation for Mama. Day to day activities consisted of school, homework, piano practice, dinner, and playing baseball in the field in front of our house. An ultimate tom boy, I often served as the pitcher on our homemade field, and climbed the big pecan tree in our front yard. At that time, a fragrant honeysuckle tree and a wisteria tree stood in the center of the trail between houses. You could smell the sweet scent every time you walked or rode by on your bike. It was just a cut-through on the way to Big Mama's house a block away.

Mama, an only child, took care of both of her parents, as well as Jerome and I. She never missed a band concert, football game, UIL event, one-act play or science fair. She always encouraged us to try anything we put our mind to and never quit. As a result, Jerome and I were in plays in the community, we sang and played at churches. I even tried out for twirler one year, although I didn't make it. One of the twirlers came to our house and helped me practice my routine. She was really nice. At that time there had not been any black twirlers. As I look back on those years, they were the best times of my life, and I don't know how she did it all. Mama took me back and forth to Austin for orthodontics appointments when I had braces, and made weekly trips for piano lessons. She took us both to the pediatric dentist in Waco for regular dental hygiene. Mama made sure we were involved and supported all of our extra-curricular activities. She never missed a football game or event that I remember. Mama was always there. Although she grew up during the Jim Crow era when African Americans were treated less than second class citizens in many cases, she never allowed those actions to make her bitter. She never projected them to us and she always said if people treat you badly, just pray for them and keep moving. God will take care of them. Mama was the smartest person I knew, even though sometimes she seemed to be hard on us. She just wanted the best for us and from us.

Mama would often make extra money through her arts and crafts over the years, whether it was sewing, making dolls, crotcheting afghans, sewing handkerchiefs, painting, macrame' lamps and more. Mama was always industrious and knew how to make a dollar out of ten cents. We never knew that we were poor. Mama made sure of it. She always told us that we could do anything we put our mind to doing.

I spent a lot of time with Big Mama. She would take me to the country when she went fishing, or to visit elderly neighbors. I accompanied her to the nursing homes where she tended to the sick and shut in. Sometimes, I just stayed with her on the weekends while Mama and Jerome traveled to our second home in Austin. By middle-school, I was no longer required to travel to Austin every weekend. I began taking piano lessons at the age of 5 and in 7th grade took up the organ with Mrs. Brown. This enabled me to get a job playing for one of the local churches. Every other Sunday, I made $20 to accompany the primary musician on the organ. This was fine by me as I didn't like going to Austin most of the time. Unfortunately, this left Jerome to go with Mama alone. It was unfortunate because Pop (Rev. Piper) was often critical and condescending and a lot of demands were placed on us as so called "preacher's kids". Nonetheless, Mama always provided a safe haven for us. Our life with Mama and Big Mama was one of security, safety, and love.

In middle school, both Jerome and I had Mama for a teacher. We were not allowed to call her "Mama" in class. We were just like every other student, calling her "Mrs. Piper." Sometimes, we thought Mama was harder on us that others. There was no such thing as late assignments or not finishing homework. My brother, in fact, learned a quick lesson as he fell asleep in Mama's class. Because he would stay up reading under his bed long after bedtime, he was always sleepy. Mama's class for him was after lunch, which made the problem worse. One day, Mama told a young lady sitting behind my brother to hold a cup of water. "If he falls asleep or starts to nod, you pour this water down his back," Mama said. In true fashion, Jerome fell asleep and received a cold dose of reality as his classmate poured the ice water down his back. That was his last time falling asleep in Mama's class.

We had good relationships with our fellow classmates and rarely experienced any problems or slights in school. Rockdale, although a small town, was a safe place for the most part. The community was tight and only a few people were known to treat us unfairly. As we got older, some kids did bully us; but, it was always short-lived. For me, a few black kids said I thought I was white and would always want to fight or pull my long hair. Being more fair-skinned with long hair was a problem for some blacks during this time. For my brother, one or two boys would gang up to steal his lunch money. It was difficult being the children of a teacher as people always perceived you had more than you did. We were struggling just like everyone else; but the expectations for us were much higher. Little did I know, that only a few short years before our entrance to the school system, Mama would come into that same school pushing down the fear and worry that plagued African American teachers who had been transferred after integration.

Mama would work daily to prove that her education and teaching style was as stellar as the other teachers who had less education. She persevered through the assumptions that black teachers and students were inferior. Yet, Mama never said a cross word to us or discussed any worries about integration. In fact, at the time, we knew nothing of integration. It was just our way of life.

Our daily life consisted of time with Mama and Big Mama. During our daily dinners, we would listen to them talk and often they would tell us about the old days. Big Mama often told stories of her childhood and siblings on the farm, as well as stories about Mama as a baby. We were safe and comfortable in that environment. Two strong women with the expectation that we could accomplish anything we set our minds to, providing us with daily encouragement to overcome obstacles. When we came home as young children crying from being bullied or hit at school, they would straighten us up, dry our tears, and help us to stiffen our backbone. I never understood why some people just didn't like us for the sake of not liking us; but, there it was.

Big Mama was funny. She always had a joke or some funny saying. Her steel blue hair and gray eyes were sharp as a hawk. Sometimes she made herself laugh so hard that she started to cry. This made us laugh too!

Big Mama would come out to play with us when we were younger, teaching us games from her childhood and nursery rhymes. She bought us one of the only playscapes in the neighborhood complete with monkey bars and swings. Her big yard became the hang-out for the neighbor kids in our younger years.

As we grew, I spent a lot of time at Big Mama's on the weekends. I began playing for New Hope Church when I was twelve, and stayed there as it was just down the street.

Mama was strict. We were not allowed to hang out in "the streets" as Mama said. Curfew was 10pm and I could not date until I turned 16. I could have company over (boy) but before that happened, the boy had to come along with his parents to ask permission. Needless to say, ha ha, that didn't happen very often. And if Mama wasn't around to keep an eye on us, the neighbors and the community always were. We had better not do anything that was going to get back from a neighbor. This included being seen on the wrong street.

When I think about all of the lessons I learned from Mama (Susie Sansom-Piper) over the years, and all of the heartache I watched her endure, I believe that her primary gift to me was not only love but perseverance, faith, and strength. Mama tried to deposit a kind word or deed into every person she met, regardless of race or color. She taught us to do the same. She kept going no matter what the situation was and she always encouraged us not to give up.

CHAPTER 16

The Years Roll By (Susie)

The third year, I met the Baptist preacher on the street, and he thanked me profusely for helping his daughter to become a better student. Three years had gone by swiftly. My life had changed dramatically in so many ways. From that point on, I knew that I would continue to make my mark in a positive way, no matter what challenge was presented to me in this new environment.

Aside from teaching, we all had special duties, which included territorial supervision of students during activity and lunch periods. Rotating during the month, we were assigned to various campus areas or building sections. We also had to work concession stands at the football games and in the gym during break periods.

To help with expenses, a snack place was operated during the lunch hour to help defray certain school expenses. Principal Lawrence always seemed to enjoy counting and examining the coins. He was an old coin collector and often traded his regular coins for the old coins acquired from snacks. I can still picture him making the boys do push-ups for punishment or giving one swat with his paddle. Even though his voice was often gruff when speaking, "his bark was worse than his bite." After a few years, he became ill, and after some unsuccessful response to many treatments in France, he passed away. He was returned to Rockdale for his burial.

After accepting the 7th-grade History position, I started to take a more active role in many other programs at the school. The same year that I took over Texas history classes, all three of the Social Studies teachers were assigned to write a curriculum guide for their respective classes. Ramona completed her 6th-grade guide. I did my Texas history guide, and in the final end, had to write the 8th grade guide for the coaches' class. I can vividly remember the Principal Lawrence era. He always tried to be fair in his way.

After Principal Lawrence passed away, we got a new principal, a coach under the principalship of Mr. Lawrence named Mr. Grindle. Principal Grindle, as a result, adhered to many of Mr. Lawrence's patterns of discipline and leadership for a time. Principal Grindle was very supportive also.

Through the years, I never really had any major problems. Twelve of my seventeen years were spent as the only Black teacher in the junior high. I made many friends among the Whites, and to this day, we are still the best of friends. Certain students made lasting impacts on my memory for various reasons. Some were good and funny memories. Others were teaching moments. Students came from all walks of life. Some were well off. Others were dirt poor. I took the time to get to know them and try to reach them all in the best way that I could.

I remember an encounter with a student while under Mr. Grindle's leadership that I will call "Clyde." Clyde had the reputation of being "Ivor, the terrible" to all of the teachers since his elementary days. I was always forewarned about the so-called "bad students." Clyde was one of my 7th-grade history students. He was a large boy, taller and much bigger than his classmates. He was stubborn, mean, and disobedient. He did just enough work to make a passing grade. On top of all of this, I discerned that he was telling his mother that I literally picked on him and singled him out. So, I decided that I would keep an anecdotal record of all of his problems and attitudes. Every time he committed an offense, I made him write it in my book, and sign it, and also date it. During open house week, Clyde's mother came to the school for the parent teacher conference. She visited my room and said that she would like to have a conference with me before leaving. I gladly consented. I later invited her in after most of the parents left and at the same time, asked her to bring Clyde with her. She did just this. I listened to her patiently. She said, "My son tells me that you pick on him all of the time." I replied, "Maybe it's the other way around. Would you like to see my conduct book?" She said, "Yes, I would." So, I began to show her the many mischievous things Clyde had done in my classroom. Next to each incident was his signature. She changed colors. Then she turned to her son and said, "Clyde, did you do these things"? He dropped his head and said, "Yes, Mom." She didn't exchange a word but quickly gathered her precious son and left immediately. The good thing is that I never had any more trouble with Clyde. Other faculty member quizzed me, wanting to know how I did it; but it was my secret. I later learned that after he finished high school, he became a prison guard with the Department of Corrections.

In later years, Allen came along. Allen was brilliant but very prejudiced. He also read, pronouncing the word Negro as Nigger. I chastised him in the same manner, but what really put a caption on the matter was the fact that Principal Grindle received anonymously the information that he had used this word. He called both of us in the conference room to find out if this actually happened. Allen admitted some of what occurred. Principle Grindle said to Allen, "I never want to hear anything like this anymore. If so, you are in serious trouble." I didn't experience any more animosities from Allen. He graduated from a prominent university in Texas some years later and became an attending physician.

One of my students was a little Spanish girl whose name was Dorothy. She was a good, average student but talkative and somewhat sassy. Dorothy was one of those exploratory students who wanted to try anything for thrills, and on the other hand, maybe some of it was peer pressure, a desire to be recognized, and to be part of the gang. One spring day, she and another young White lady decided to play hooky from school. They stayed home and invaded their parent's liquor cabinet. By the time they returned to school, they were both very inebriated. They went to the P.E. class, and the P.E. teacher thought that they had been physically molested from their actions. Shortly afterwards, she recognized the problem, put them under the cold shower, and immediately took them to the office. They remained in class, pending a conference with their parents. After learning about the situation, I decided to try to take Dorothy under my wing and just talk, talk, and talk to her. I pointed out her good points and encouraged her to develop her potential. After Dorothy finished her junior high years, she still corresponded with me.

I'll never forget two students who gave every teacher the "blues." Keith was disrespectful, unruly, and couldn't get along with the other students. He chewed tobacco, reportedly used alcohol and drugs, and was the typical epitome of the "bad boy." I was forewarned, "He's tough," "He's hard to handle," and "You'll never make it with him." Teachers had been having trouble with him ever since he was in 2nd grade. I just smiled. Most of the teachers kept him in the front seat. They were expectant of the things he did. They called themselves 'being prepared' by keeping him front and center. Keith was always in the office for something he had done.

I always seated my students in alphabetical order, so with this arrangement, Keith was about midway in the room. My first few days of school were always spent talking to my students. I never expected anything special from them, for all that I ever asked was for their respect and to do their work in preparation for future life. Keith was fine the first week but, afterwards, began his usual antics. I would always keep him about five minutes after class, sometimes in the room, other times in the hallway, and just talk with him about his behavior and how it would affect him in later life. Somehow, I won him over, for I never had to send him to the office for punishment. He was not an "A" student, but he did average work. He did graduate from high school. In searching background information on Keith, he was given everything by his parents that he desired, including a motorcycle. A few years after high school, he was killed in a motorcycle accident.

The other student was Diana, a bubbly little White girl. Outside of my history class, Diana spent most of her time in isolated study situations. They had tried moving her from teacher to teacher with no avail. She talked incessantly and often played pranks in school. This meant that upon recommendation of the teacher, because of behavior problems, the student was given assignments and placed in the hallway isolated settings to work on her lessons.

Diana was talkative and posed a problem at first, but I also kept her after class many times just talking with her. What Diana really needed was love, someone to care what she did, and someone to believe that she could achieve. She relayed to me that she had a home but seldom saw her parents. She lived with her stepmother and father. When she left for school in the mornings, they were asleep. When she returned home in the afternoon, they were leaving for work. So, there was little to no personal contact. She could leave home in the afternoon and return when she got ready. Most times, very late at night. She was a 13 or 14-year-old girl on her own. When her report card went home with bad conduct grades or failing grades, and a conference was required, her parent's reply was, "We didn't know." I worked with Diana all during her 7th grade year. We became not only teacher and student, but I was her confidante. The more we talked, the better she began to act.

And then there was Randy. Randy was partially in regular classes and in Special Ed. Actually, he was everyone's problem in a way. He was disobedient, impotent, and disrespectful. From meetings with his parents, I would say that being the baby in the family, he was just spoiled. His parents never really believed that he was a troublemaker. Randy was a regular student in my Texas history classes. He decided that he was going to "cut-up" in my room. I corrected him in the classroom, but since that seems to have had no effect on his behavior, I decided to begin using my "after class for five minutes" talk with him. I don't really recall all of the things we talked about, but whatever I said caused him to improve his behavior in my classroom and to do enough work to pass. Unfortunately, after going to high school, he kept up the same pattern of misconduct. He finally ended up robbing a local grocery store and receiving time in the penitentiary. After his incarceration, he corresponded with me for many years. He expressed regret for his wasted years and the conditions he was now experiencing. I wrote him to encourage him, but, in later years, I lost touch with him.

I can remember when Donald told his father that I had called him a lie in the classroom. In my 41 years of teaching, I never called any student a lie. I may have said something in the manner of "you're not telling the truth," but not called someone a "lie." But to complete the story, Donald's father came to the school to "jump on me" or "beat me up" for calling his son a lie. He threatened to throw me down the stairs. Principal Grindle met him at the entrance and, like Mr. Lawrence in previous years, told him he would be in serious trouble if he entered the school. He attempted to argue, but my principal won the battle, so to speak.

There were also those who furnished joyous times in the classroom as well. Candy was a tall, lanky girl who was always full of fun. When we discussed the Texas Longhorn Cattle, the students had to draw pictures of the Longhorn. Candy's picture was well-drawn, but she definitely wanted everyone to know that her cow was a lady. She placed a big bow ribbon between the horns. That was the funniest thing to see. I kept that picture as a reminder for me of her class.

Robert was full of antics. At the beginning of school, he wanted his little locker to be "home-like." So, he found a piece of carpet to place in the bottom of the locker and hooked up a battery-operated lighting system so that he would have lights. Then he invited me to see his book's home. I stifled a smile as I complimented him on his creativity and ingenuity.

There were the Cooke brothers, Ken and Kevin. Their work was always unique in illustrations. They were excellent artists and often drew their illustrations for their various projects.

During those early years, campus activity was separated. The girls played on one side and the boys on the other. We had football and basketball teams, as well as junior high track. Girls played half-court basketball with six-man teams, plus substitutes. There was no communication between the girls and boys. It was particularly a No-No for any Black boys to talk to a White girl. Somehow, this was sensed and often unspoken. Each stood off in his own little niche: the Whites, the Hispanics, and the Blacks. At this time, the girls were beginning to wear the short-short dresses, so we had a dress code on the junior high campus. If your dress did not reach a certain length, you were sent home to change or given a three-day suspension until you could comply.

There was limited participation during the early years in any school functions, with the exception of sports events. In previous years, in the all-Black school, cheerleaders, Majorettes, etc., had active parts in school activities. Selectees in the integrated school were chosen by student votes, passing grades, etc., and since whites outnumbered Blacks 5 to 1 in every way, those who tried out didn't have much of a chance. It was equally hard for Blacks to make the honor roll. I can remember an experience encountered by a high school student whereas when report cards were received, a point or more had been sliced from their grades. Luckily, her parents had kept all of her test papers, and the teacher in question had to retract or redo the grade.

I always provided homework on a weekly basis, and I always felt that there was ample time to complete it for the next week. I either made copies to pass to each student or wrote assignments on the blackboard. I always made my history classes a learning and fun process. We made scrapbooks depicting life of the early Texans, made tombstone rubbings of early pioneer gravestones, made studies of the various nationalities who settled in Texas, and during Black History Month, we inserted a study of famous Blacks and made a scrapbook to keep. Since no Black History was being taught, this was a way to introduce students to Black History. One year, we got another Black teacher at Rockdale Junior High. Ms. Lille A. and I first initiated a Black History program. We carried out this program for two years. She presented one year, but the following year, she went to another school in Dallas to teach. I was once again the only Black teacher in the school.

My third year, the school hired a school counselor. Her name was Ms. L. I had been certified and tested as a counselor for years, and I was passed over for this role. The counselor they hired claimed that she would do all of the testing. I was not even considered. This was one of the many slights that happened throughout my career I did find that there seemed, at times, to be more prejudicial behaviors than experienced in those first years of integration.

Within six years, one big accomplishment was the organization of the UIL program for Rockdale Schools. Our elementary and junior high schools only competed on the district level. The first year, I set up the program and trained the 7th grade spelling team, which incidentally won the blue ribbon. The winners were Julie B. and Maria G. The next year, Tommye and Tamara (Tammy) were winners. One year, Ken C. was my poetry representative in UIL competition and won the blue ribbon with his rendition of "Mending Wall" by Robert Frost.

Although most days were routine, there was still an air of acceptability on what we could and could not do as Black teachers. They really did not want you to teach anything about Black History in school. I worked with Lillie, the counselor, one year to have a Black History Program. The one year was actually all that could be arranged. After Mr. Lawrence died, and Lillian left, I went to Principal Grindle to get permission to present the Black History program during the month of February. He really did not want to allow anything to do with Black History. His reply was, "If you present a program, then we'll have to allow the Germans, Mexicans, etc., to bring in their programs. So I will have to say no."

I was not disheartened, but I felt that this should have been permitted. During earlier years, a National Negro History Week had been set aside in February by the late W.E. Dubois. In later years, the entire month of February was designated by Congress as Black History Month. The reason for this was because there is very little information written in the textbooks pertaining to the numerous contributions and inventions of the Black race.

I respected his wishes but was determined to help present to my 7th-grade students a phase of Black History. So, I incorporated a six-week program beginning in the month of February into my curriculum. I requisitioned film strips, gathered more Black magazines, and gave special research assignments on famous Black people. It was interesting to the children and amazing to the whites. They would often express, "We didn't know, or we thought this or that…" I had collected a numerous amount of material pertaining to Black History.

That year, I also had a portable machine that operated by battery at home. I used my machine to show films regarding Black History. I kept it in the very top back of my closet and would take it home daily. The kids really enjoyed this information. The next thing I knew, I received special magazine subscriptions and records. I still have the information and magazine subscriptions that I used to teach this information. I received notes and letters from some parents during this time, thanking me for teaching their children about Black History.

It was apparent that over the years, we had to prove ourselves, and *strange* as it may seem, we did just that! The first-grade teacher became known as the "best first-grade teacher," and parents began requesting for their beginners to be placed in her classroom. The Special Education teachers produced worthy students who could accomplish enough to meet approval to survive and finished high school. The science teacher, Mrs. Petty, became one of the top science instructors in the United States, producing many, many outstanding science fair winners. For the next 16 years, her students excelled in the Regional and International Science Fairs. They went on to make history by winning the Regional Science Fair sixteen times and International fourteen times. These students won many trophies, savings bonds, medals, scholarships, and other recognitions. My granddaughter, Tamara, was the first in Rockdale history to begin this long pattern of success. Laura was her Biology teacher. Laura became a member of the Regional Science Fair Board, served two four-year terms on the International Science Fair Advisory Board, two years as Secretary of the Advisory Board, and two years as Chairman of the International Science and Engineering Fair (ISEF) Forum Committees.

She received more than 300 special awards, including the Texas Engineering Award from Austin and Texas A&M Universities and the Family Award TANDY (one of 100) Top National and Science Teacher Awards featured in Time and Fortune 100 in 1992. She also earned a Ph.D. degree from Texas A&M University and, after retirement from Rockdale High School, taught Texas Adults and Needy Families (TANF) at Blinn College. After 29 years in the public schools, she retired in 1994, only to return in 1995 and become the first African American to give the graduation address to Rockdale graduates.

I became Chairman of the Social Studies Department at Rockdale Junior High, UIL Organizer, and was selected as one of the top Texas history teachers in the country. In later years, I trained poetry speakers of which there were many winners.

Most people began to get used to segregation, and the students that started to come later had only been to an integrated school. Students came and went, some successful, others not so much. And so, the years rolled on…

CHAPTER 17

Broken Windowpanes

Elizabeth Keebler-Ross said "People are like stained glass windows. They sparkle and shine when the sun is out, but when darkness sets in, their true beauty is revealed only if there is a light from within."

Reflecting on this beautiful quote, one might venture into an opposite direction by saying, life is sometimes like broken windowpanes. It breaks into numerous pieces, and before it is mended, it is sometimes stuffed with rags, papers, or cardboard.

The lives of the young men that I will present have been akin to broken windowpanes, and for some, the panes (pains) have been replaced. Others seek replacements that never let the light shine through. One might wonder in what direction is the writer traveling?

Several years ago, some of my former students had taken a pathway plagued by drug use. They eventually stole, robbed, prostituted, sold drugs and more to maintain their lust. Some went to jail, while others ended up in the state prison system. Some of them wrote me numerous letters, and I in turn, replied or sent them the monthly church newsletter.

I had often wondered what happened to these individuals. Most of them came from good homes where they were lovingly supported by their parents. Why did they turn to drugs? The idea came to me to do a survey, so I wrote to those in prison, asked questions, and through them, I was introduced to others prisoners who were lonely for mail or just someone to talk to. After their release, many went to half-way houses to try to mend their broken window-panes (pain). They had a story to tell. My request was to use only pseudonyms to protect innocent persons.

L.J. Was a college student at Sul Ross University. He came from a stable home and had one sister. After entering college, he had a desire to make fast money to supply his needs and buy new things. So, LJ began to sell drugs. He was an active participant in all ports in high school, and a member of the science club. He said, "growing up, my life was smooth sailing". He told me that his "actions and habits placed me in jail, but I managed to escape the prison life, because my parents showed me that they really cared for me." LJ said that he had he knew he should have listened to his parents, teachers, and stayed away from the drugs, but the fast money, fast life, appealed to him and contributed to his downfall.

Then there was Don. He held a BBA degree with a concentration in accounting from McMurry College. Don says that before he got into trouble his life was pleasant. He had a lot of activities and participated in sports, was initiated into a fraternity, and was a member of the judicial counsel. Then the pane in his windowpane of life broke. He began associating with the wrong crowd, because in spite of all of his activities, he says, he was lonely. First he was caught with cocaine, then he was caught operating a motor vehicle under the influence of alcohol. To satisfy his cravings, he would maneuver himself into situations where he could get drugs for free. This entailed giving free rides, or making connections for other people. His life broke into pieces. He lost all sense of integrity and his ability to enjoy life seemed to have vanished. Don says that he only wanted to associate with the drug crowd, and he had no room for growth. He lost his family. He didn't want to go home and he became anti-socIal. He just wanted to spend time getting high.

Fortunately, Don didn't go to prison, but entered a rehabilitation facility. He became determined to change because he felt that he owed this to himself, his family, and community. Don said "You must realize life is a struggle, and without a struggle, there is no gain and there is no growth. Anything that is gained in the fast lane is not worth it."

Next was Darryl. His parents lived in a beautiful brick home. He was a high school graduate and an active participant in sports. He was by all intents and purposes, a star athlete. After high school, he worked a little, but had a strong desire for life without rules. Darryl began to hang around the beer joints, drink alcohol, and do drugs. To support his drug addiction, he lied to his parents about needing money. He would beat or cheat young drug dealers out of their products. He would tell them that the police came down on him. He even stole from his parents and others that loved him. Darryl says that he had "no conscious". His addiction kept him on the streets and out late at night. His eating patterns changed and he began to look bad physically. Drugs, Darryl said, changed his way of thinking, causing him to feel that everyone was out to get him. His life was normal up until 1988 and that is when the downward slide began. The introduction to powder cocaine took Darryl on a downhill slide.

Dee Dee's windowpane of life broke into very tiny pieces. After high school, he says that he began a normal life, working, and soon having a family. He got into drugs and his family could not stand to see him in the condition he was in. He lost his wife and children because he never had money for them. He soon ended up in prison. In 1992, a female undercover agent executed a drug buy from Dee Dee. The agent bought 6 bags of crack cocaine. Six months later, he was walking through the doors of the county jail. He ultimately received a 40 year sentence because he was already a convicted felon. In one of his letters, Dee Dee said, "Mrs. Piper, I remember you always telling us to 'believe in yourself and you can make it'. This is so true, because you have to to believe in yourself to make it in this place. He asked that I deliver a message to the younger generations in churches, homes, and schools, and that is to stay away from drugs, gangs, or anything related to crime. Per Dee Dee, it is very hard to get out of prison, and it is difficult for inmates to survive from day to day without getting into trouble. "So please tell them to stay in school and be all they can be." Dee Dee is still repairing his window pane. He learned the chalkboard rules but started to apply them too late.

The next individual I corresponded with was an honor high school graduate. He was a talented actor and singer. He was cited as being outstanding in drama. His high school accolades merited him a full scholarship to a prestigious university. Like others, he came from a very stable home and had a strong religious foundation.

Unlike some of the others, he was trained and encouraged to work at an early age. While growing up, he often kept elderly people's yards, and later began working at the local fast food establishments. He was not a deadbeat, nor did he depend on his parents. Most of his immediate needs were available. The question I have in all of these cases is what went wrong in their lives?

The answer is the same, peer-pressure, self-esteem, desire for riches, and people recognition. BJ says life was good before he got into trouble. He was trusted by people and comfortable with himself and the things that he participated in before drugs.

When he went to college, he encountered a lot of peer pressure. Somehow, he felt as if he was not accepted y people outside of his immediate family. Being a part of the crowd, over-rode his desire to uphold his personal standards and the values he was raised with. He didn't want to be called square and he joined a crowd to support his acquired drug addiction. This led him to steal, forge checks, lie and con virtually anyone he could get to. Eventually, drug dealers threatened to eliminate him and he ended up spending a year in prison. This came after many visits to the county jail. BJ said that he tried to convince himself that he was comfortable with his choices, but in reality, he only felt good about it when he was high on drugs. When he came to himself, he became very depressed. The drugs caused him to lose so much- his family's trust and real friends. He remembered my teaching as well, "Don't be afraid to stand up for yourself and the beliefs that you know are right, and stay away from people that you know are doing wrong". He said, don't be concerned with what people say about you especially because you are trying to do the right thing.

Finally, I spoke with Joe D. He had just been released from the Texas Department of Corrections. His plight, background, and desires were very similar to the others. He cited disobedience to his parents, teachers, and just wanting to do things his own way merited him a drug addiction and several years in TDC.

Joe D said "I learned a lesson that is not taught. The world keeps moving and you are not a part of it when you are in prison. You only have to sleep and eat. You incarcerate your entire family because they sacrifice to try to help you. The friend you ran with are nowhere to be found. You only have God to help you bare the burdens and when you have good parents and people who still care and support you, it's a great help.'

When I reflect on these students and the path they traveled, I am thankful that these are just a few that followed the wrong road. There are so many many more that have made their parents, teachers, and community proud. But all are worthy of love, compassion, and concern. Thinking about past years and times gone by, I often contemplate the fact that prior to integration, there was not the proliferation of drugs available, nor the numbers of people addicted to substances. Now, I do not suggest that integration caused the epidemic; but, it seems that when the community was tighter, more involved, more cohesive, the number of addicts, prisoners, and others were much less. Of course, drugs have always been around, from heroin, marijuana, and LSD use in the 1950's to the 1970's to the burgeoning cocaine use after integration. The perplexity of life experiences of today make me wonder what happened to yesterday. Many years have gone by. Unthinkable living conditions, expanded beliefs, and concepts have emerged leaving me to ponder the future in a difficult world. As my thoughts wander to and fro like ocean waves, I think about what happened to traditional ways, good manners, respect, and stable ways of life. Those days where one could take a walk in the park, children could play outside without supervision, one could walk down the street at night without fear of being robbed or accosted, raped or murdered for any unknown reason. Families gathered for the evening mean, dining, chatting, and enjoying one another's company. The broken window panes in my story had those opportunities, that stability, but strayed. Now the broken window panes are not just those that have been incarcerated, but also those that have left common decency and self-respect by the wayside.

I try to picture myself in my younger days, as a teenager. I couldn't see me wearing a skirt so short that you could see the seat of my underpants or a blouse cut so low, that the only thing remaining to be seen are the nipples of the breast. As for young men, pants sagging so low and loose displaying their under shorts, leaving anyone watching fearful that they will eventually fall to the ground. I thought about my teenage and college years. No designer clothes and two pairs of shoes. One for school, the other for church. The garments we did have must be kept clean and neat.

Thinking about the window panes in my classroom, teachers in the public schools were losing respect. Now, teachers endure abuse from parents and students. In the past, a teacher could hug a student, give them a pat on the back for encouragement. Now, it is not so. If you do, you could be accused of sexual harassment or child molestation. When scolding a student for wrong-doing, you could be accused of abuse or harsh language. It comes to me that these are the things that began the cracks in our windowpanes before they broke entirely. What happened to common decency, good manners, pride in dressing, respect for others and self?

CHAPTER 18

Teaching Can be Fun

O ver the years as time passed, I would occasionally have the student, parent, or colleague that I could tell did not like blacks; but overall, every school day was just another day.

My trusty notebook helped me to keep track of the misdeeds of students and because I set the rules and expectations up front, there was no question about how to behave. I often think this was something that was expected in the black community because those of us that survived integration had similar control in our classrooms. I remember my colleague Mrs. Petty was also known for being a stern and fair teacher. Talking in her classroom, much like mine, was not allowed unless students were given permission to speak. Her favorite saying that students repeat to this day is "Class, I have a low -grade interference in the room." That meant it was time to be quiet.

In my class, projects were always the high light of the year. Students were required to draw or model the Texas rivers, the longhorn cow, and other markers of Texas history. One of my prized possessions was a drawing of the longhorn by a student named Candy. Candy was an amusing but kind child. When it was time for the class to present their drawings, Candy had artfully drawn a longhorn with a bow ribbon on its head. I don't know why to this day, but that was the funniest thing to me and I kept that memory throughout all of my years.

Next there was Robert. Students in the past were assigned lockers to hold their books and various personal items. Robert had a talent for flair. When assigned his locker near my classroom, I noticed that it was artfully colorful. Robert had placed carpet and other fabrics in his locker, lining the walls and base, along with a mirror and various other sundries of colorful and sparkly items. He had the most fashionable locker I saw over the course of my career.

Each year while teaching Texas History, I had the students bring exhibits of the food eaten in olden times, models of cabins and teepees, and other exhibits that represented the history in Texas. I loved seeing the creativity of the students. Some brought cooked items like hot water cornbread and chili beans. Others made drawings of the Texas rivers or plains. Sometimes the cornbread was pretty strange looking. But, as the teacher, I had to sample and enjoy the products from my students and grade their efforts.

At Christmas, as teachers often do, I received numerous presents from my students. Before the break, I was often loaded down with brightly colored cups, homemade cookies, fruit cakes, bells and various trinkets, little figurines, and pretty much everything else you can imagine. Sometimes I received letters from my students over the break. Tons of cards from current and former students and parents filled my mailbox. I loved hearing about the accomplishments of my students, and their plans for winter break. I would often be so overrun by tins of brittle and cookies, that I shared the treats with my neighbors and anyone who stopped by. I began a bell collection from all of the various bells I received and my students began collecting them from different locations that they traveled to. Today I have hundreds of bells of all different shapes and descriptions.

Throughout the years of teaching, I have counseled, supported, and educated thousands of students. I have watched more football, basketball, and other games than I can remember. The entire community showed up for sporting events and we all celebrated at the prowess and winning spirit of our students. There is something different in the air of a small town when all of the citizens are gathered for one purpose. While there was sometimes division, many people began accepting the newer way of life and the generations coming behind did not display the same prejudicial behaviors for the most part as those who came before. During my teaching career, I thought long and hard about the joys of teaching. I jotted down things that make a successful teacher who can impact students positively throughout their lifetimes. I thought about the legacy I wanted to leave for my students and the advice I would give to new teachers.

Many writers have said, "A teacher is forever". This is an acceptable quote for teachers are forever. A child's formal teaching begins with parents in the home. When they reach the daycare, pre-school status, a new experience in the learning process is begun. Reaching the kindergarten level simply means that the child has become of an age to relate to new learning experiences that will determine his/her future in the society in which they will live.

Who Am I? I am your school teacher. I am the open-door to your future life. Your teacher is many packages wrapped into one. Teachers are your parents at school, mentors, counselors, sculptors to help you identify your talents and refine them. Teachers are your nurses or doctor if necessary, idealists, representatives, and advocates, lawyers, and friends, and yet they have tremendous responsibility of imparting knowledgeable information for your learning process.

The teacher in those who teach and those who once taught is an on-going part of life that includes some of their concepts, experiences, and encounters from their career, which can also help their students to achieve a measure of success. A dedicated teacher has the interest of her students at heart. They develop a secure relationship with them, merits their respect, and yet maintains good discipline in the classroom. A good teacher is fair in decision-making, realizing that each pupil, regardless of the number in the room, is a different individual, with a different personality, and a different level or pace of learning. This dedicated teacher does not stereotype their students; but, always remains encouraging to those who are great achievers, as well as to those who struggle.

When, where, and how, should I begin my journey in the teaching profession? The dedicated teacher always tries to become acquainted with parents of the students, letting them know that they are interested in their children. The first week of school is really "get-acquainted" week, and especially with the students. Good teachers set expectations and guidelines. Good understanding makes teaching an easy process. Remember that all children will "try the teacher", just to see how lenient, fair, or far they can go to get away with things. Once a student is allowed to get a head start in the discipline process, one will begin to experience difficulties. Be aware of the fact that children are very much like adults. They want attention! Many children do not receive attention at home and as a result, they are seeing that "something" that will boost their self-esteem. Recognize them when they do well, and recognize them when they don't do so well. How? Use encouraging words, such as this is good; but we will try to do better next time. A tiny encouraging message written on their papers has a tremendous effect on their attitudes. Your pleasant and encouraging attitudes somehow rubs off on them.

From a personal viewpoint, I share the Five R's...

R- Reading- Learn to read well, for reading maketh a full man.

R- (W)riting- Write legibly and be able to express yourself in a written form that can be readily understood.

R- (A)rithmetic- You must learn numbers to a degree where you can handle your future finance successfully.

R- Respect- Always respect yourself first, and it will not be difficult for you to respect others.

R- Responsibility- It is your responsibility to try to learn and to be a success

Preparation, dedication and responsibility are keys to being a successful teacher.

PUT-patience, understanding, and tolerance are inclusive to all teachers. As one teaches, always remember why you became a teacher. Realize that there is joy in teaching, for the student is like a bud, and it is gratifying when you see them blossom into a beautiful flower. There is a measure of self-fulfillment. Just think! What you put into the lives of others will someday come back into your own.

It is so fulfilling for me to see and meet students that I taught many years ago! Many times they still remember my teachings or something I said that resonated with them. My greatest desire in teaching is to help others set and obtain goals. Obstacles would come but during my career, I had to always remember that there is something inside each mind that could be developed, and sometimes, one has to search for it. All students would not become engineers, doctors, scientists, or teachers etc., but if through my teaching, your teaching, you can see the outcome of a future "good citizen", and member of society, you have done an excellent job!

Last, it is always important to be a good example for the students to follow. Attitude, manner of dress, conversation, etc. is often imitated, even if you are not aware of it. A teacher is a reflection in the mirrors of the lives taught each day! Yes, a teacher is forever!

CHAPTER 19

My Treasures (Letters and Notes)

The most precious and heartwarming treasures to me are the many letters and notes I received from my students over the years. As a history teacher, or any teacher, you never know what you are depositing into the lives of the many children you encounter. When I met a student on the street or received one of the hundreds of cards and letters over the years, I can look at my life's work and be proud of depositing just an ounce of fortitude or knowledge into the lives of my students, my children. These are just a small sample of the notes I received over the years. They are my most valuable possessions, my treasures, the legacy of my life.

• •

"To the one, we, the class of 1989, love the most, you, Mrs. Piper.

****

I would like to wish you a very Merry Christmas and a Happy New Year. I really hope you enjoy it. Sorry that we can't see each other the weeks that we have free, but we both have family that we need to spend this wonderful time with. Just remember that we all love you a lot. You really did teach us a lot, and I don't just mean about history. But you also taught us respect and a lot more. Stay sweet, and keep your head high. And you'll go far. God Bless you. We all love you.

Merry Christmas and Happy New Year

Love,

R.H."

• •

"This wonderful lady was not my teacher, but she was the same generation as my teachers. I taught and loved the two grandchildren she was raising because their mother had died. I still stay in touch with all three. In 1975, I was a second-year teacher coming off a rough first year and went to work at a new school for a principal who openly admitted that he "hated band directors." For some reason, this magnificent lady "adopted" me and encouraged me constantly. I am honored to be her friend and colleague, as well as someone she mentored. The writer of this article, the editor and publisher of the Fredericksburg (TX) Standard, was one of my all-time star band students. He says she was and is his favorite teacher, and I am happy to be in her shadow. (By the way, a few years later after that old principal retired, he confided to me that I was the

only band director he ever learned to like. He would turn over in his grave if he knew I told anyone he said it.) Thank you, Susie Piper, for a lot of great memories of those years.

J.P"

D2 | March 21, 2018 | 𝔉𝔯𝔢𝔡𝔢𝔯𝔦𝔠𝔨𝔰𝔟𝔲𝔯𝔤 𝔖𝔱𝔞𝔫𝔡𝔞𝔯𝔡-ℜ𝔞𝔡𝔦𝔬 ℜ𝔬𝔰𝔱

Yes, my favorite teacher is a national treasure

Texas Type

Ken Esten Cooke

March is Women's History Month. February was Black History Month. Readers, allow me to share the story of a black woman who continues to have a profound influence on my life — my former teacher, Susie Sansom-Piper.

I was a fuzzy-headed 12-year-old when I had Mrs. Piper for seventh-grade Texas History, and I was largely unaware of the racism and strife that had plagued our country only a few short years before.

In the classroom, Mrs. Piper was firm, but fair, and always encouraging.

As I got older, I learned that Mrs. Piper had been the last principal at Aycock School, the school for African-Americans before desegregation. As I got older still, I realized she probably would have been a better administrator than many our district had over the years, but she was likely denied that opportunity because of her race. Yet we students never heard a cross word from her about it.

She finished her career and lived in our hometown a while before moving to east Austin. There, she became active in her new church and in other civic work.

In 2016, Mrs. Piper was chosen by the LBJ Library in Austin to speak at an event honoring the 50th anniversary of our 36th president's signing of the Voting Rights Act. She was joined by Luci Baines Johnson, a familiar face around these parts, who praised Mrs. Piper for her teaching. (Remember, her father began his career as a teacher.)

Luci Baines Johnson also talked about the political capital and sacrifice it took just to allow the Voting Rights Act to pass. "Some of these members won't be coming back here (Congress) because of their votes," she remembered him saying. "But he told me a lot of good people in the future would be coming here because of this vote."

Mrs. Piper lived through the days of poll taxes, intelligence tests and other roadblocks to African-Americans gaining the right to vote, a century after emancipation.

In 1965, only three states still had a poll tax — Texas, Alabama and Virginia. Not the Lone Star State's proudest memory.

In her speech, Mrs. Piper brought along a poll tax receipt, dated Dec. 29, 1964.

Susie Sansom-Piper

"You had to pay the poll tax to vote," she said. "It cost $1.75. You could feed a pretty big family for several days on that."

She also recalled that teachers and employees of the school district were told who were the preferred candidates of the powers that be, and that they were expected to cast their votes accordingly.

Other impediments to vote included the migratory nature of adults and children, who had to follow the seasonal work in the cotton fields to make ends meet. Transportation to and from the polls was yet another problem.

She summed up her talk by saying the Voting Rights Act provided many treasures in her life, including "the privilege of voting for the candidate of my choice," adding "choice, not of coercion."

History, warts and all, is what she taught. At age 12, we had no idea of the obstacles faced by our classmates and their predecessors who happened to have darker skin.

Today, Mrs. Piper continues to teach, write a column each February for Black History Month highlighting local contributions from African-Americans, from business leaders, to military veterans, to city council members, to entertainers. It goes without saying that many, or even most, of those stories would have been left undocumented and lost forever had she not taken the time to document and share them.

She also has written several books of thoughtful poetry.

A couple of weeks ago, my family joined her friends from St. James Missionary Baptist Church in Austin to honor her at a surprise party. Now 96 years old, Mrs. Piper continues to be spry, still working on her church's newsletter and playing organ at times.

Many shared their memories of Mrs. Piper.

I read an editorial written by our hometown newspaper editor Mike Brown which tabbed her as a "national treasure." I told the crowd everyone should be so fortunate to have a teacher like her. And every community should be so lucky to have someone like her telling the stories of those often overlooked.

She was, and still remains, my favorite teacher.

ken@fredericksburgstandard.com

March 21, 2018

Yes, my favorite teacher is a national treasure

By Ken Esten Cooke

March is Women's History Month. February was Black History Month. Readers, allow me to share the story of a black woman who continues to have a profound influence on my life — my former teacher, Susie Sansom-Piper.

I was a fuzzy-headed 12-year-old when I had Mrs. Piper for seventh-grade Texas History, and I was largely unaware of the racism and strife that had plagued our country only a few short years before.

In the classroom, Mrs. Piper was firm, but fair, and always encouraging.

As I got older, I learned that Mrs. Piper had been the last principal at Aycock School, the school for African-Americans before desegregation. As I got older still, I realized she probably would have been a better administrator than many our district had over the years, but she was likely denied that opportunity because of her race. Yet we students never heard a cross word from her about it.

She finished her career and lived in our hometown a while before moving to east Austin. There, she became active in her new church and in other civic work.

In 2016, Mrs. Piper was chosen by the LBJ Library in Austin to speak at an event honoring the 50th anniversary of our 36th president's signing of the Voting Rights Act. She was joined by Luci Baines Johnson, a familiar face around these parts, who praised Mrs. Piper for her teaching. (Remember, her father began his career as a teacher.)

Luci Baines Johnson also talked about the political capital and sacrifice it took just to allow the Voting Rights Act to pass. "Some of these members won't be coming back here (Congress) because of their votes," she remembered him saying. "But he told me a lot of good people in the future would be coming here because of this vote."

Mrs. Piper lived through the days of poll taxes, intelligence tests and other roadblocks to African-Americans gaining the right to vote, a century after emancipation.

In 1965, only three states still had a poll tax — Texas, Alabama and Virginia. Not the Lone Star State's proudest memory.

In her speech, Mrs. Piper brought along a poll tax receipt, dated Dec. 29, 1964.

"You had to pay the poll tax to vote," she said. "It cost $1.75. You could feed a pretty big family for several days on that."

She also recalled that teachers and employees of the school district were told who were the preferred candidates of the powers that be, and that they were expected to cast their votes accordingly.

Other impediments to vote included the migratory nature of adults and children, who had to follow the seasonal work in the cotton fields to make ends meet. Transportation to and from the polls was yet another problem.

She summed up her talk by saying the Voting Rights Act provided many treasures in her life, including "the privilege of voting for the candidate of my choice," adding "choice, not of coercion."

History, warts and all, is what she taught. At age 12, we had no idea of the obstacles faced by our classmates and their predecessors who happened to have darker skin.

Today, Mrs. Piper continues to teach, write a column each February for Black History Month highlighting local contributions from African-Americans, from business leaders, to military veterans, to city council members, to entertainers. It goes without saying that many, or even most, of those stories would have been left undocumented and lost forever had she not taken the time to document and share them.

She also has written several books of thoughtful poetry.

A couple of weeks ago, my family joined her friends from St. James Missionary Baptist Church in Austin to honor her at a surprise party. Now 96 years old, Mrs. Piper continues to be spry, still working on her church's newsletter and playing organ at times.

Many shared their memories of Mrs. Piper.

I read an editorial written by our hometown newspaper editor Mike Brown which tabbed her as a "national treasure." I told the crowd everyone should be so fortunate to have a teacher like her. And every community should be so lucky to have someone like her telling the stories of those often overlooked.

She was, and still remains, my favorite teacher.

ken@fredericksburgstandard.com

CHAPTER 20

The End of an Iconic Era: Just an Old-Fashioned Teacher

In 1982, my eldest grandchild, Tamara graduated from Rockdale High School with honors. Each of my three oldest, had received $10,000 Texas Achievement Scholarships to the University of Texas in Austin (Tamara '82, Cynthia '83 and Jerome '84). After Jerome graduated, I decided it was time to retire.

I reflected on the transportation years. My oldest had bought a little Chevette with money she earned from playing for church and a little job at the local donut shop. She also played piano to accompany many of the UIL solos for band students, often being paid $5 per solo. Tamara inherited the Samsonite luggage her mother had taken to Prairie View A&M in 1959. Her clothes were mainly homemade with a few bought in between. I thought about our trip to Prairie View with our daughters in 1959 and how different the trip to the University of Texas was 17 years later. Her first year was in Jester Hall, which I called the maze. She had a radio, television, and the bare necessities. Fast food and dormitory food was available. In 1984, with the graduation of my grandson, Jerome, I decided to retire.

The patterns and priorities of parents began to change. All or most of the parents wanted their sons and daughters to be in the spotlight. In spite of it all, under the new regime, I was reprimanded for "giving too much homework" because the baton twirlers didn't have time to practice their twirling, or the cheerleaders did not have enough time. When the principal said that I gave "too much homework" and "his daughter didn't have time for her *extra-curricular activities*," I decided it was time to go. I decided I had had enough when parents were more concerned about extracurricular activities than the education of their children.

When I was ready to retire, many parents begged me to stay on.

I had collected a substantial amount of material on Black History and left it for the next teacher to use after my retirement. It was somewhat disappointing to learn that at the beginning of the year, most of this was classified as "trash" and thrown away. This was passed on to me by another history teacher. The film machine I used was also left at the school when I retired.

In the years that I served at Rockdale Junior High; I was always given excellent ratings but never superior. However, the parents of the students, when encountered, always recognized me as a superior teacher. They recognized me as one who understood children and presented to them incredible learning experiences, not only in printed matter, but provided them moral values and goals to attain.

Some things stick most in my mind as successes during my tenure. Reaching those students who were deemed unreachable is a treasure to anyone with a heart to teach.

I walked the halls of the now new Junior High and reflected on my many years in the classroom. I packed my things, all of the many gifts showered on me by my students and parents, and walked into the next phase of my life.

As was my way, I wrote a letter to my students, my final class.

"You are my final classroom students.

As your Texas history teacher for the year of 1983-1984 school year, may I say that I'm glad you passed my way.

We both have learned, for we shared together the lessons each day, the behavior problems, and most of all, that if you desire to be a success in life, it is necessary that you must put forth your best effort and WORK!

I sincerely hope that you have learned not only something about the state of Texas but that you have learned the principles that we talked about all year. These principles will last you for a lifetime…

Do you remember them?

1. *Listen*
2. *Obey*
3. *Respect (for self and others)*
4. *Responsibility*
5. *Study*
6. *Be honest.*

Remember to always strive to do your best in whatever you undertake to do."

With love,

Mrs. Susie Piper

A Teacher is Forever."

• • •

Over the years, I ran into them in stores, at church functions, or when I would come back to visit. My reward was always to hear from them how I touched their lives or just to know that they learned something from my class. Children grew up and had families. Lives changed. I loved hearing their stories and seeing their growth. Sometimes, I remembered them when they greeted me, and sometimes I did not, but they were all special, just the same. Of the thousands of students I taught, some always stood out for their stories, their classroom antics, or their accomplishments.

One day, years later, I met Dorothy in a local grocery store, the young girl who played hooky and came back to school drunk. She hugged me and said, " I have you to thank for helping me to see the light. I'm a secretary now, and I work for the Education Agency". It's things like that that made all of those teaching years worthwhile.

Several years after retirement, I was visiting or shopping at a Target store when suddenly someone called my name. "Mrs. Piper, Mrs. Piper, don't you know me? I'm Diana." Diana was the young girl that I had helped and talked to, as she was often home alone. She had put on a few pounds, but the voice was familiar. She gave me a big bear hug and said, "I've longed to see you. I just want to tell you I did finish high school, and I have a good job at I.B.M. But most of all, you helped me to believe in myself and turn my life around!" I felt like shedding tears, for I really couldn't think of anything special that I had done.

There were many others who may have been problems in their own way, and there were some who did well in school and conduct but, in later life, made many mistakes which caused them to have to pay penalties. Many of my students have turned out to be great contributors to society and very successful in their own rights.

I have just been guilty, I guess, of having a love for all the children I've ever taught. The good, the bad, and the ugly, and it is gratifying to me when they turn out A-Okay! All some of our children need is encouragement and someone to care. Alternative schools and special education are not always the answer.

As I reflect on my life in the classroom, I think about the many students that have crossed my path and the tremendous accomplishments some have contributed to society. I am just an "old-fashioned teacher." Today's children have every conceivable modern piece of equipment in and out of the classrooms, and yet they are left behind. They cannot perform simple mathematical skills or read, write, or spell sufficiently. One may ask why I would make such a statement. In former years, one had to learn mathematics and read well, even if you were made to read aloud in class. You had to memorize multiplication tables for there were no calculators, and you became so apt in these skills that you could go into a store and total your bill in your head without pencil or paper. Writing skills were a must, as well as correct spelling. These days, I even see teachers who cannot spell. How are they teaching when they use simple words with incorrect grammar and spelling? Memorization was important.

In 1988, I editorialized my opinion in the Rockdale Reporter on desegregation (20 Years Later). May 1988 marked the 20th year of "complete togetherness" in the Rockdale ISD, and special recognition for the great measure of success in uniting the minds of our young people is to be given.

Good times have not always been foremost. There have been trials, tribulations, feelings of despair, mixed emotions, feelings of rejections, shed tears, but the same has been exemplified throughout the nation.

The end results have been most excellent, for the learning process shared by parents, students, and teachers have produced a spirit of unit of purpose. "What is best for our children"?

Reviewing 20 chapters of history (1968-1988) of the desegregated RISD, one can readily reflect and be proud of the success of our youth. As in the "melting pot", they have blended their talents together to produce a school system that is recognized nationally.

As a former teacher in Rockdale Junior High School, there are fond recollections of the experiences that I encountered. But through it all, the fact remains that all children need that special kind of touch, that special love, and special care, that only we, the people, united together for a common cause can give them.

Susie Sansom Piper

I was never really sure of the effect of my teaching and my blackboard maxims had on my students until 1993 when the late Aycock High School honored me with a presentation of my life during the school reunion. To my surprise, there was a page called Memories of the Blackboard. There were my blackboard rules listed.

As I often have the opportunity to encounter children in various situations, it leaves me wondering what they are being taught and how. A few days ago, a 5th-grade student came by to sell something for a fundraising event for his school. He had not been given any instructions, presented only the catalog, and had not filled in his information as a common courtesy. Old-fashioned me invited him inside, set him down, and had him complete all of the necessities for his salesmanship. Then, I gave him some instructions to present to the next person he encountered. A few days later, I went to a local café in South Austin to eat. A 4th-grade teacher had a display of short stories on a huge bulletin board. Old-fashioned me began to read as I waited in line. There was a display of poor sentence structure, poor spelling, and incorrect punctuation marks. Old fashioned me was almost tempted to dig in my bag, get a red pen, and begin circling the errors that should be corrected. Then I reminded myself that this is another world, and I was just an old-fashioned retired teacher. In this hurry-up world, there is still enough time for good instructional skills, and if properly initiated, no child will be left behind. Some of the students who were labeled as hopeless candidates for society and renounced later succeeded. In my years of classroom teaching, I did not hesitate to correct students so that they could learn. I always believed that there was some learning capacity in every student. The names are fictitious, but here are their stories.

I met Will during my first day of teaching. In 2002, Will wrote me a letter. He said " My fondest remembrance of you is when I was in the fourth grade. I always felt rejected and that I didn't belong with other children because my environment was so different. You taught me how to write my name correctly, to be good in numbers, and then to sing. You developed my self-esteem and a belief that I could be an achiever. The years have gone by, but I just wanted to say thanks. " Will was being reared by his grandmother who was old at the time, and a mother who suffered from mental problems. He became a gold medal winner in voice, and a college professor at Grambling State University in Louisiana.

Then came Antone. His mother was killed in an automobile accident. There was no father in the home, so he was being reared by his older siblings. Because of his acute mischievous ways, Antone was often taunted by some of the teachers with their words. They would tell him that because of his behavior, he would never amount to anything. His family history and background played an integral part in their words. Antone then came to my business classes and became and efficient typist. He was brilliant enough to be salutatorian of his high school graduation class. He joined the armed forces after high school and retired from the military. He always said because of my teaching, belief in him, and persistent encouragement, he had a most successful service career, training and traveling all over the world. All of his work was in the administrative offices. After his retirement, the government employed him to be a Chief over government affairs in Germany and France.

In 2006, or 22 years after my retirement, I met one of my Hispanic students in the Rockdale Walmart. He saw me in the aisle, called my name, and made me recollect him. Jimmy introduced me to his family and then said: "I'll never forget you, and especially those things you would write on the blackboard. I use them to discipline and encourage my children." I thanked him and then thought to myself, 'I guess a teacher is forever'.

In 2017, I went to a reunion with my granddaughter, Tamara. I was overjoyed to see many of her classmates and to hear how they made a difference in the world. One young man, I will call G, came up and hugged me. He said "When I was in your class, I hated you. You were the meanest teacher and made us do so much work. Now, I am a sheriff and I can reflect on the teachings you gave us and I appreciate you so much!." This was the funniest thing to me. I thought how blessed I am to get this feedback and to see one of my students who had achieved so much and spent his life being a public servant, both in the military and as an officer.

When I remember these students, I often think of today's challenges. I thought of the parent who wanted to sue a teacher because she used a red ink pen to circle her son's errors. She said that it made him have low self-esteem. I have often wished that I could inject some of these old-fashioned ways of teaching into this modern society. When I see what is happening in society today and see some of the steps we are taking that appear to be moving us backwards in time, I recognize that we still have a long way to go. A long, long, way to go in education and how we treat one another. As much as I would like to believe that racism was overcome, it still exists in the hearts and minds of some people, and it saddens me to know how far we have come but still need to progress.

CHAPTER 21

The Second Act

After I retired in 1984, I toured many schools illustrating Black History information and how Texans lived. I did some substitute teaching in the Austin area occasionally, but focused my attentions on writing and helping out in the community. My Mama was still living in Rockdale so I still made the weekly trip home to buy her groceries and catch up on the local happenings. I received many accolades and honors for my work in the community and in schools. Although I retired, I did not quit. For a few years, I did intermittent substitute teaching in the Austin Independent Schools but soon decided that I was done with the classroom. I decided to focus on sharing my gifts in other ways in the communities.

I moved full-time to my second home in the Austin area, although for many decades, I traveled back and forth to Rockdale and still conducted business there. I continued to write annually in the newspaper and made the trip to converse with old friends and check on Mama. I facilitated numerous speaking engagements in the Austin area and shared my knowledge and writings with anyone who cared to hear. Most of my writing outside of the newspaper have been focused on spiritual inspiration. I have numerous religious documents, authored and edited the church newsletter, and have peened several books, including *Tied to Mama's Apron Strings, When A Loved One Dies,* and *From Valleys to Mountains.*

Although my mama went on to her heavenly destination on Christmas day 1990, I held on to the Light Bread Hat that adorned her head on many occasions. I hung it right over the desk in my office. Her Light Bread Hat remains a decorative item in my home. Whenever sadness or unfavorable conditions invade my life, or if I need a source of inspiration, a look at this hat gives me the needed comfort. This is a legacy of simplicity but a valued treasure that is sustaining and carries a weight of security as I go about from day to day.

The LADY BY THE SIDE OF THE ROAD

She lived in the house by the side of the road.
    On a corner where two streets meet.
    And as all mankind passed swiftly by,
    Kind words to each, she would greet.

Her nimble fingers sewed many garments.
    Her tender touch pulled the teeth of tots.
    The giving spirit…the loving kindness,
    Spread cheer to many lots.

No matter how small, tall, rich, or poor,
Her tender hands embraced each.
To all who chanced to pass her door,
Within her loving reach.

And when the curtains of her life,
Began to close its sheers,
The life she lived for all mankind,
Brought job and love for her fruitful years.

@1990

Time moved forward. The kids were all grown and I now had a great granddaughter. She was my only one. In 2004, I accompanied my only great-granddaughter, Brittany to her move in at Southern University, in Baton Rouge, La. I am just an old fashioned teacher. I have transitioned three sets of children to college, and followed the path of many of my students. What a change in 2004! It was amazing to see the parents driving up in cadillacs, jaguars, and plenty of SUV's. Quite different from our 1950 Ford on the campus of PVAMU. Most amazing to me was the unloading. TV's, computers, DVD's, radio's, cell phones, refrigerators, regular phones, microwaves, all sorts of food, shoes- especially tennis shoes galore, and more. When I observed the dress wear, it appeared that anything goes.

Freshmen were not allowed to bring their autos the first year. The flower children years had passed and a complete revolution of ways of living seemed to have emerged. Yes, I was just an old-fashioned teacher, and times were rapidly changing.

In 2015, I was honored to speak at the 50th anniversary of the federal Voting Rights Act, which President Lyndon Baines Johnson signed into law August 6, 1965. I shared the dais with his daughter, Luci Baines Johnson, sharing a poll tax receipt dated December 29, 1964. You had to pay the poll tax to vote. It cost $1.75. You could feed a pretty big family for several days on that. At the time the Voting Rights Act was signed in 1965, only three states still required a poll tax: Texas, Alabama, and Virginia. The poll tax was one impediment to voting in the African American community before 1960s-era civil rights legislation.

My address at the LBJ Library:

REMEMBERING POLL TAX AND VOTER REGISTRATION

To all that's present, and especially to Bruce Elfant, Travis County Tax Assessor- Collector and Voter Registrar; to Mark K.Updegrove, Director of LBJ Presidential Library; and to the beloved Luci Baines Johnson, who was with her father when he signed the Voting Rights Acts some fifty years ago, and to all that's present today.

What a thrill for me, and what a privilege for our present young generation, for you have the freedom to make your selections of personnel; and life's privilege to continue making our world, a world that can promote and enjoy happiness.

WEBSTER DEFINES CIVIL RIGHTS AS THE RIGHTS TO PERSONAL LIBERTY ESTABLISHED BY THE 13TH AND 14TH AMENDMENT TO THE UNITED STATES CONSTITUTION AND CERTAIN CONSTITUTIONAL ACTS.

Our late President Johnson said: "The right to vote is the basic right without which all others are meaningless."

Before 1964, this definition was only words written in the textbooks to be read by America's students, and practiced only by a specific race of people. An integral part of the Civil Rights Acts included the right to vote.

Voting for individuals to occupy certain offices during this era, was relegated only to one race of people. One may readily ask the question: Why?

My home town, Rockdale, Texas is a small country town, located 60 miles east of Austin on Highway 79. This is where I had my beginning, my work, and my overall living until retirement.

1. Many Blacks did not vote because of economic conditions. During those days, many had to follow seasonal work in the cotton fields just to survive. Many children did not get to enroll in school at the beginning of the year, because of this work schedule. As a result of this migrant work status, voting and educating oneself about candidates were not a paramount concern in the community, because people were trying to eke out a day- to day existence in the early 50's

2. There was a $1.75 poll tax, the amount required to register. This amount could feed the average big family for many days back then, and besides they had to save money for the winter months, but, as a teacher, we had no choice but to register with the $1.75 fee, for we were expected to cast our vote. Oft times, we were, as teachers, and employees of the school district, "told" who the "preference" was, by the "powers that be", and were expected to cast our vote accordingly.

3. Most people did not have adequate transportation, nor news media to learn about the importance of voting. So, efforts or knowledge had to be passed on by word of mouth, schools, churches and other organizations that existed on the other side of the tracks.

Though many became eligible for voting, due to the aforementioned factors, few actually followed through with the voting process in my hometown. Yet, their cohesive vote produced the first Black Council member of the city of Rockdale in 1978, and every election since that time, has produced additional Black Council members.

How did these changes influence my life?

The Civil Rights Acts has provided many treasures in my life:

- *The privilege of voting for candidates of my choice*
- *The power to expressing myself through the written power of words, without fear of repercussion.*
- *The ability to live and enjoy the best of life without fear of retaliation.*
- *The ability to accept being a victim of choice and not of coercion.*
- *The ability to have successful ventures and great self-esteem.*
- *The ability to honestly believe that My Vote, My Voice and My Opinion, matters.*

Yes, it was August 6th, 1965, when our Honorable President Lyndon Baines Johnson, passed out 75 pens to 75 supporters of this great Civil Rights Edit.

Thus began a new beginning and a new way of life for all American Citizens.

So let us embrace the privilege, and encourage Voter Registration among all eligible citizens.

Susie Sansom Piper

August 6, 2015

I also spoke for the League of Women Voters at the premiere in Austin of the movie <u>Suffragette</u>, starring Meryl Streep. Suffragette was a graphic depiction of the suffrage movement in the early 20th century Brittain, where political activists fight for equality and women's rights to vote. After the move, I sat on a distinguished panel to discuss voting rights with the League of Women Voters.

I continued to play for my church choir, the Goldenaires, at the St. James Missionary Baptist Church until April 2019.

I have had the pleasure of meeting and conversing with many former students since my retirement. I think about the children they once were and the people they have become. Not all become great successes. Some have weathered tragedies, and a few have been incarcerated. I have received letters from prisoners ruminating over the lessons they received in my Texas history class and the plans they intend to set in motion once free. I have met others who remember something from my blackboard, or some funny incident related to the projects I required as homework.

As I listen intently, my heart smiles as I remember the common thread in all children, regardless of color, is concern. They all want someone to listen, pay attention, support and love them. For in this way, I did my best. My gifts were profitable, and I have been richly rewarded with many "Thank You" letters and memories. It always warms my heart to meet a former student and hear the wonderful things that they have done in life. Children don't learn hate unless we teach it. Babies don't come out hating other babies. Toddlers don't see or feel disdain for other colors. It is a taught and learned behavior. To me, all children need love, and a good teacher, a *great* teacher, will show them how to be greater versions of their best selves. Help them to hone their skills and help them to find their way. I am grateful to have been given the opportunity to contribute to society and to ALL of my students. For this is the legacy that I have been blessed to be a part of, and through education, one lives forever.

Some of the sentiments shared with me stay with me forever and allow me to know that my life's work was not in vain include the following:

- One student I paddled in 7th grade actually thanked me for paddling him, for it made him a better man.
- Another time, I met a family at a café, and they hugged me and thanked me for the principles that I taught their children because it helped them to become better, more productive children.
- I also received a letter from the editor of a newspaper indicating my influence on student's lives.
- Another of my students said that my teaching him to type saved him from being on the frontlines of the military. He was able to keep an office job because he could type 80 words per minute as a result of my Aycock typing class.

These and many others who stop by make my life meaningful as I have sown into the lives of thousands during my tenure.

I mentioned in the foreword some of the great friends I made in the public schools. I have also been blessed to meet great friends in the Milam County Community. Those that encouraged me, helped me and cheered me on to tell stories of the former students of Aycock and their accolades. The former students that shared their successes and allowed me to write their many stories. The students that became my surrogate children in a sea of many - some closer than others. I won't strive to name them as I will leave someone out, and I LOVE THEM ALL!

I thank the Rockdale reporter for printing my Black History and other series every year for over 45 years (*"Way Back When," "The Other Side of the Tracks,"* etc.). Mr. Cooke, Mike Brown, and many others not only encouraged the series, but gave me an outlet to educate and uplift others over the years. I am thankful for that opportunity and friendships. I often hear from former Rockdalians many states away who have read about a former classmate or friend. As a small community, Rockdale has generated legacies of greatness in all races. For this, I am so very proud.

I also thank Citizens National Bank, formerly Rockdale State Bank. For after the loss of my husband, people like Virgie T., Carol T., and others helped me to learn management of finances (as a widower). I had never really had to take care of the financial end of our household, and after my husband's untimely death, everything was left for me to handle. These citizens and friends helped me to weather the storm. Their foundation with me has led to life-long friendships and a strong relationship with Susan and others at CNBC today.

To my community and family, near and far, although I list you last, you are definitely not least. As my eyesight dims and my health wanes, I want each of you to know that you are special. The *Other Side Of The Tracks* in Rockdale, a once full and vibrant community, is now a shell of its former self. The ancestors are long gone, and the younger generations have moved to Austin and other surrounding communities or other states. Your jobs are bigger, your houses are newer, and you can travel the globe, unlike the days of segregation. Unlike the days of the Green Book, you/we can pretty much go anywhere you want. It is so unlike the days not so very long ago, where some states and areas and hotels were off limits to African American citizens and bi-racial couples were against the law. This is a blessing.

I am proud and happy to see from whence we came and where we are going. I came from a tight-knit community. I came from a close family of Moultry's and Crayton's. Many aunts and uncles, and first cousins who were raised with me like brothers and sisters. One casualty of integration is that families became more educated, had better access to education, and moved further away. This, in turn, has created more distance between the family nuclei. As our elders, and now my generation, has passed away, our children, grandchildren, and great-grandchildren, in many cases, rarely see and barely know each other. The legacy of camaraderie and fun, family support, and the sharing of meals has dwindled to gatherings every few years and strained connections.

Share the stories of your ancestors. I pray that all of you and your offspring continue to prosper and pay it forward. Pull together, even though time may be short and distance between you may be far. Tell the stories that you remember. Educate your children, grandchildren, great-grandchildren, nieces, and nephews the way it was and the way it will be. Without sharing the stories and the history, we lose touch.

I have been blessed and fortunate to know my two great-great-granddaughters, Kianna and Brianna. They teach me new technology, like how to work my new cell phone, YouTube, and Snapchat… and *I* teach them about our history. But, as we continue to move forward and technology becomes more and more advanced, it is incumbent on us to knit our families together. I pray that our families and communities will once again draw closer together, rely on each other more, and show today's children the meaning of family, communication, and friends.

As of August 23, 2019, at the age of 98, I committed myself to completing the story I started all of those years ago of my *Seventeen Years in the Black Room*. My granddaughter, Tamara, transcribed the book through my many notes handwritten over the course of 60 or more years, and the stories I told them as they were growing up. Some of the pages were written on that very first day in the classroom. The paper is now yellowed, frail, and brown. Lines are smeared with the remnants of my salty tears. The tears I shed in the quiet moments when no one was looking. Tears I shed in the nighttime when I lay alone with my thoughts.

Sometimes, there was turbulence through the years. I have experienced tremendous sufferings, not bodily sufferings, but mental trepidations. In my later years, I was blessed to give a presentation to the grief committee at my church on how to overcome. I listed my encounters as Pandora's box, which contained grief, depression, worry, loneliness, financial woes, sorrow, greed, hatred, anxiety, self-pity, and jealousy. But through steadfast belief in God and prayer, I have endured and overcome. I adopted the motto: "I will be tough on the outside, yet tender on the inside. Then walk with character, integrity, and lift my head high in the face of difficulties."

The long-ago poet Edgar A. Guest vividly expressed for me what others don't know about me. He began by saying:

> *I have to live with myself and so*
>
> *I want to be fit for myself to know.*
>
> *I want to be able as days go by*
>
> *always to look myself straight in the eye;*

It has always been my desire to be a role model for those who follow after me. I made it through my faith and determination to produce and succeed. I have never desired a spotlight position, but just hopefully portray or leave a legacy to emulate.

Through it all, I have been tremendously rewarded. I treasure my memories, my lessons, and the life I've lived with many of you. To my students, always do your best. What you sow into the lives of others will someday come into your own.

As my breath grows short, I say to you," Never, Never Give Up! Never Quit! Never Stop Moving! For when you stop, your life is over"!

Love To You All-Always,

Susie Sansom-Piper

• • •

Reflections

Reflections are like capsules of time
Focusing on happenings of the past
Captured in visionary images of life
Cherished by present generations and generations to come

Reflections are like beams of light
Bouncing on surfaces of days gone by
Producing thoughts of events that were
And Meditations of a future yet to come.

Susie Sansom Piper
March 2004

CHAPTER 22

Mama, the Latter Half, Through My Eyes

My name is Tamara Suzette Hebert Powell. I AM the granddaughter of my beloved Susie Sansom Piper. Mama named my brother and I. She was my hero, my teacher, my inspiration. Even through the writing of this book, I spent many hours reading her handwritten notes, journals, newspaper articles, and treasures As I read through her writings, I not only felt more of a tremendous sense of pride, but honor, and gratefulness that I had the opportunity to be raised by this tremendous woman of humility, accomplishment, and compassion.

Strong in will and slight in stature is how I would describe Mama through the latter half of life. As I became an adult, she was my advisor, confident, and road buddy when I traveled between Austin and Baton Rouge our any where else I needed to go. Much like life with Jerome and I, Mama never missed a football game or road trip to watch my daughter Brittany in the high school band. She made every concert and school activity. If I was going, she was ready.

Mama still drove the highways well into her mid-nineties, and really only slowed up because Jerome served as her driver most days. It was nothing for her to pop up at my house in Round Rock having driven herself the 20 minutes across town. I would often chide her gently that the traffic was too bad to be driving whereas she would proceed to advise me that she had been driving almost a hundred years, and besides, she took the "back way".

Not only did Mama help me to raise my own daughter; but, she was also blessed with two great-great granddaughters (Kianna and Brianna). Not many children can say that they were around to see their great grandparent, much less a great-great. Mama delighted in the girls. They were her hearts. She often kept Kianna while I traveled for work, and they wore matching night bonnets to sleep in. On Wednesdays, she and Jerome would pick up Kianna from daycare and they would go on their weekly outing to CiCi's pizza or McDonald's. She would spend the night with them and in the morning, there was always fresh pancakes for her breakfast. In keeping with her character, Mama penned a series of stories about Kianna on each of her first six birthdays. It was complete with her family history, antics, and memorable moments. These are treasures that she will have forever.

In 1997, Mama buried her second husband, Rev. John Piper. She had nursed him through lung cancer for 18 months while also caring for Big Mama who now had breast cancer. I remember praying that Mama had so many tragedies in life that the remainder of her life would be filled with friends and the ability to do whatever she wanted. As the years progressed, I watched as church members, former students, and friends rallied around Mama. She was taken to dinner, events, plays. She attended various outings with former students. She was often called upon to speak or write speeches at the various churches. She threw herself into penning the church newsletter for twenty five years. Growing up, I saw Mama as serious and pensive. She was stern and matter of fact. Now I know that there were so many things on her mind. So much turmoil, and she just kept putting one foot in front of the other. As the great-great grands came, I saw Mama smile and laugh much more often. My daughter Brittany, "Miss B" as Mama called her had grown up and now had two girls of her own. Mama was much more light-hearted, although I could still tell when she worried. Occasionally, she would cry. Throughout everything, Mama always told us to have faith in God. As such, the years passed swiftly.

I remember the August that Mama stood before a crowded room in her vibrant blue skirt and blouse. My brother accompanied her on this day, as he often did. Age had shortened her stature, but her commanding presence still existed nonetheless. She shared her remembrances of the signing of the Voting Rights Act into law 50 years earlier. At 94, she was still busy teaching every opportunity she received. She took this and other opportunities to educate others, encourage younger people, and continue to exhibit her demeanor of strength and dignity throughout her life. After the event, I accompanied her to the premier of Suffragette with the League of Women Voters. I marveled as the audience sat mesmerized at her sharing of the pride she felt in voting, and the challenges African Americans and women overcame to have the right to vote. She encouraged the young women in the audience to be dedicated, not become complacent in the privileges we have today. She also talked about her days of registering others to vote. Mama told the audience that our ancestors overcame many obstacles to have the right to exercise the liberties of all Americans. We sometimes become complacent and entitled. She offered this as a reminder that we all have a responsibility to live up to the legacy our ancestors secured, and to pass on the same sense of pride and respect to future generations.

As I look back over my own life, I marvel at the many things that Mama did and am grateful for the example she provided us. I am proud of the legacy she left and of the history she gave us about who we were and where we came from.

Mama still played for church, drove herself to church every Sunday, and never really missed until my brother passed away Thanksgiving 2018. When he died, I saw Mama begin to wilt before my very eyes. Her resolve, her will to live changed that day. The death of another child was more than her heart could bear.

Mama was the strongest woman I knew. She had more fortitude than anyone in my life, male or female. I had the greatest pleasure of not only growing up with her; but, also being by her side during the last six months of her life. Those days gave me a different perspective and insight into the woman that I called Mama all of my life.

During the last six months of Mama's life, I began transcribing her story, Seventeen Years in the Black Room. I realized that she had been writing this story over many years and found numerous tablets with similar versions of her first day in the Black Room. It became clear to me that this was the most profound and defining moment in her life and all of her thoughts were directed towards capturing those moments. It was then, as I went through her writings, that I saw the vulnerability and pain of integration. I saw the resilient spirit that I had known; but, from a different perspective. I saw the tear stains on the brown fragile paper between notes and sentences written many decades before.

As a student during integration, I never realized the struggles Mama had in the Jr. High after integration. I only saw the strong accomplished teacher with the clickity clack heels that commanded respect from all of us, her students. I didn't see much of the differences between us and other students as I had gone to an integrated school from kindergarten. I never knew that when I was chosen to play piano and accompany the choir in the Junior High Christmas play or when I sang in the quartet with my classmate Tommye or that she, her brother, and mine, were the among the first black Gabriels and soloists in the pageant.

Yet, at home, although she told us stories of history, she shielded us from many of the slights and discriminatory acts that might have come our way.

In the fragility of those last few months, I saw the young woman who outlasted segregation and integration. The woman who made a place in the world that was uncertain for many African Americans; a woman who was an only child; a caregiver who persevered and exhibited great strength, one who raised two small children in her early 40's, buried two husbands, nursed and buried both parents, a daughter, an uncle, and a grandchild- all alone. Who was proud of her family history and legacy on both sides. Whose grandfather was a settler in Rockdale before Rockdale was a town. Who came from a legacy of firsts and established a standard for firsts in our lives. All of these things flashed through my head in those final months.

In August 2019, two months before her death, I had the great opportunity to take Mama to the African American History Museum and the Holocaust Museums in Washington DC. She had become frail and I wasn't sure that we would make it; but, in true Mama fashion, she rallied and made the flight to DC. I hired a driver to take us to the main sights and Mama was able to comfortably ride from one museum to another. Over the years, I had often traveled to DC but due to the demands of work, it was difficult for me to take her with me. This time, I knew I had to make it happen. This was the opportunity of a lifetime to see the world through Mama's eyes.

Mama seemed transported in time as she told us about the Jim Crow Law, which began in 1877. They were enacted when the Supreme Court ruled that states couldn't prohibit segregation on common modes of transportation such as trains, streetcars, and riverboats. Later in 1883, the Supreme Court overturned specific parts of the Civil Rights Act of 1875, confirming that separate but equal concept. The Jim Crow laws were a number of laws requiring racial segregation in the United States. These were enforced in different states between 1876 and 1965. Mama's memory at 98 year's old was impeccable, and she recited the history for our benefit. Jim Crow law provided a systemic basis for segregating and discriminating against African Americans. Common laws included literary tests and poll taxes, and other restrictions on voting meant to keep black men from casting a ballot. There were also bans on interracial marriages, and separation between races in public places of business.

Mama expressed her sadness that in many ways, we as a nation seemed to be going backwards. Some people demonstrated less compassion and pride in their families. Some minorities failed to vote, a privilege that black men and women fought hard to get.

She talked about the Civil Rights Act which legally ended discrimination and segregation instituted by the Jim Crow Laws, followed by the 1965 Voting Rights Act which ended efforts to keep minorities from voting.

I marveled at how my loving grandmother, my Mama, at the age of 98, still had such a strong mind, remembered stories of her past, and how she gave us instructions on how to live in the future. Mama said: "One casualty of integration is that families became more educated, had access to better education, and moved farther away. This in turn has created more distance between the family nucleus and the community. As our elders, and now my generation has passed away, our children, grand-children, and great-grandchildren in many cases rarely see and barely know each other. The legacy of camaraderie and fun, family support, and the sharing of meals has dwindled to gatherings every few years, and strained connections.".

She said that we should share the stories of our ancestors. Pray your offspring continues to prosper, and pay it forward.

Each time I pick up another journal, a small piece of paper, or the back of an envelope from Mama's things, I find a new story, saying, or thought. She was constantly writing the story of her life and words of encouragement to leave as legacy for years to come. As I prepared for the writing of this book, I reminded myself that eventually, I had to cut off the information. The legacy Mama provided and the historical references she left would fill more books than a lifetime. Far more than I could ever include. These notes and journals provide new gifts of discovery every day.

CHAPTER 23

Mourning a Legend

In her last days, Mama often talked while I wrote and recorded her words. She was adamant that Seventeen Years in the Black Room be told, published and shared. There is so much more to her story, but it has taken me four years to be able to get to a point that I could at least put a pen in it. I only pray that as you read, you learned, you shared, and you found nuggets like I have from some of the many stories I heard directly from Mama over the years. For 42 years, Mama provided historical information and writings to the *Rockdale Reporter* during the month of February during Black History Month. This hometown newspaper and the family who owned it, embraced diversity when it wasn't popular and probably at times was not prudent. I am grateful to the Cooke family for their friendship and willingness to embark on this journey that lasted nearly a century. Mama always sought to tell the truth and also focus on the positive attributes of African Americans from Milam County. She told stories of triumph over tragedy, accomplishment over adversity, and perseverance over pettiness. For many years, she spent her time writing about the great accomplishments of many of her former students and her love for the Rockdale community.

Before dawn on October 21, 2019, my life as I knew it ended. For the past six months, I spent every single day with Mama. Talking with her, cooking for her, laughing with her at stories of her time in the classroom, and crying with her over the loss of my brother Jerome, who passed away Thanksgiving night 2018. The grief of his death took her strength and weakened her resolve to make it to age 100, as Jerome always said she would. Mama regaled me with the stories of her *Seventeen Years in the Black Room*. Sometimes, I typed as she talked. There were other days that I worked to transcribe her handwritten notes from long ago and asked many questions. Sometimes, I recorded short videos while she talked.

A little over one week earlier, Mama had taken to her bed. Her legs no longer willing to hold her. She gave me a list of former students that she wanted to speak with, and I called them as she wished. On October 17, they began to visit. I worked in the other room, marveling at how strong and vibrant Mama sounded. Calling me periodically to grab this or show them that. She spent an hour or so talking to each as they came and went. She sat up in bed, although in pain, she showed none of her apparent weakness. She regaled them with stories and instructions for after her demise. Like the queen she was, Mama held her own through each visit. I reflected back on how she commanded attention in her classrooms from the minute we heard her footsteps walking down the tile laid halls of the old Rockdale Junior High. Her high heels making a clip clap as she walked towards the classroom. The closer she came, the quieter it got - if you were smart. For two days, I witnessed that same valor and strength. Shortly after each would leave, she would tell me she was in pain. She might eat a little or simply go to sleep.

On Saturday, October 19th, I had to bring in a hospital bed. Mama's bed was too high and too large for me to continue getting her up. On that day, I explained that I needed to move her bed so the nurse and I could get to her. I knew the time was coming to a close as she was barely eating and had ceased eliminating. She asked me why and I gently told her that her system was shutting down. A number of close church friends were there to see her that day. When I walked into the room, Mama grabbed me and squeezed me so tight that I could barely breathe. She was still strong. I couldn't fathom that we were at the end when she had so much strength. hugged her back tightly and cried. "I love you, Mama; I don't want you to go," I whispered. She just kept squeezing me, smoothed my hair and called me Mama's baby. She whispered she loved me while someone patted my back.

After she let me go, Reverend Lewis and his wife Letha, helped me to sit her up. He gently put her socks on her feet and helped me move her to a chair while the men in the room disassembled her bed. Tears streamed down my face. I was so grateful for all of their presence in this moment. As we got Mama into the chair, she raised her both of hands, looked towards the sky, and exclaimed, "I love you, Lord! Thank you, Lord! I love all of y'all! I love all of y'all." We love you too, everyone in the room expressed. On my knees, I laid my head on Mama's lap, and she patted my hair.

I had to leave her sitting up for a little while until they brought the hospital bed. The entourage from earlier departed, and I was left with Mama, my husband Marcus, and a dear friend that grew to love Mama from her hospital stay. As the bed was assembled, she helped me get Mama into bed, and Mama began to sleep. Mama had stopped speaking when she called out to the Lord and expressed her love for us. Her breathing now became raspy and labored. I placed an oxygen cannula on her to make her more comfortable and took my place in a chair at her bedside.

On Sunday, more church members she loved came by. She lay quietly as they spoke to her or sang to her. Her skin, wrinkle-free and translucent. I called my daughter Brittany and the girls to come and say their goodbyes. They made it in the early evening and sat at her bedside for a few hours before heading back for school and work. My friend Tommye came from San Antonio that evening with food and offered to stay up with me that night. She, too, sat with me at Mama's bedside for several hours before I told her I would be okay. She hugged me as she left Mama and I to solitude. After locking up, I settled into the ladder-backed chair at her bedside. A soft orange light dimly glowing in the room.

On that last night, Oct 20, I began to read to Mama. I picked up my computer. "Seventeen Years in the Black Room" by Susie E. Sansom-Piper. *"For the last 22 years, the question has been repeatedly asked of me: what was it like during the integration years? How did you make it? The next statement is always, if someone doesn't tell us, we will never know. I am 'Someone,' and this is my story."*

I read the legacy she had written over the years as my eyes filled with tears and spilled down my cheeks. My voice shook and wavered as I promised her that I would finish the story, her story, this story, and make her proud. I looked for a sign, any sign that she was hearing me. Her breathing had become labored, and her eyes teared ever so slightly. She never moved. Her last act had been the day before when she grabbed me in a vice-like hug and told me she loved me. I cried as I knew this was the time. The room was quiet except for the sound of my soft voice, the raspy rattle of her breathing as death moved in to overtake my Mama, and the constant hum of the oxygen tank I had added the day before to make her comfortable. I kept reading. Sitting there alone with her in her dimly lit yet peaceful room. I believe that she heard me. I prayed that she did and was pleased. When I finished reading, I slowly closed the laptop and vowed again to finish the book soon.

I tried to lay down for a while, but I couldn't, so I took up a post at the other side of Mama's bed and began playing all of the classical music pieces that she loved to hear me play over the years. She had spent so many years taking me back and forth to piano lessons, and I became an accomplished classical pianist. Granted, I stopped regular practice years ago, but I promised Mama I would start practicing again. As I played each song, she seemed at ease. Although her breathing began to get louder, she didn't seem to be in any pain. At 5:40 a.m., Mama opened her eyes. She blinked, but she didn't speak. She was perspiring, so I changed her nightgown and wiped her forehead. Her eyes had turned an opaque gray, and I knew she was not seeing me. "I love you so much, Mama. Please don't go. You're my hero." I cried. Mama blinked a few more times. She took a few deep breaths and stopped. I couldn't believe she just stopped the raspy breathing. I turned on the overhead light and took her pulse. I laid my head on her chest and cried. Mama was gone. I tried to dry my eyes and sent a text to the hospice nurse. "Alana, my grandmother, Susie Sansom Piper, is gone." I then readied myself to start making calls.

Mama took her final breath, and the vibrancy of my hero, the brilliant light of my Mama, dimmed. The commanding schoolteacher voice of a legend in her own right was silent. Although I knew the bigger-than-life impact that Mama had on the lives of my brother and I, as well as many from our small town, her far-reaching impact became even more evident in the days and weeks following her death.

I wondered why I hadn't finished the book before that day. Why was it so hard to complete before she passed away? Why did God let me spend so many weeks working on the revision for *When A Loved One Dies: Principles of Steering Through Grief*? I believe that all of those weeks of writing and study were preparation for this very moment when I would be without my beloved grandmother, the woman who raised me, nurtured, and protected my brother Jerome and I. She was the mom who attended *every* concert, football game, and band event. She never missed an award ceremony, a recital, a pageant. This was the woman who didn't take sick days. The mother who made sure we were cultured by taking us to museums and plays, procuring private piano lessons, concerts, and recitals, reciting our family history, instilling a sense of pride, and ensuring we faithfully attended church every single Sunday. My mother transitioned right before my eyes.

When Mama passed, there was such an outpouring of love and support from our home community (Rockdale), the Austin community and church family (St. James Missionary Baptist Church), and from people all over the world that Mama taught or touched. It was a that moment that I realized why I hadn't finished the book before her passing. The last chapter was her legacy. The many wonderful stories told by her students and people she impacted was the end of the book. I set out to capture as much as I could because this was such a representation of her. The last chapter, her last chapter, was the seeds she sowed into others not only in the classroom but also in her everyday life.

Mama would often ask me what she had done to garner the praise and accolades that she was fortunate to have received during her lifetime. She was a teacher, historian, mentor, and compassionate advisor wherever she went. More than anything, she loved people, and she never quit. It is with gratitude and humbleness that I share the words of some of her students from her many years of teaching. It was Mama's most ardent desire that she leave something positive with everyone she encountered in some manner. I believe that her legacy is not only everyone that she touched but everyone that may be inspired by a little lady who, at the age of 98, still wrote books, played the piano for her church choir, shook her finger when you got out of line, and gave instructions to some of her most precious students until two days before her demise. Susie Sansom-Piper lived a life of fullness and abundance, triumph over adversity, and faith in the face of tragedy. The lessons she left will endure for many generations to come. Although she left this earthly home, she left me with a lifetime of love, lessons, and history, for which I will forever be grateful.

It has taken me four years to put the finishing points on this book. At each review and every time I sought out to write, I faltered. I was not sure if it was good enough, wondering what else Mama would want me to write. If there is one thing, I gained even more so from the review of her writings and the history of our family is a great sense of accomplishment and pride. Gratefulness for being the granddaughter, great-granddaughter, and great-great-granddaughter of people who mattered. People who stood for excellence. People who loved people. Although four years have passed since her departure, it feels like yesterday. Mama was my hero. She was my everything, and today, I lay the pen at rest to submit a small portion of her work to you. I am hopeful that in this work, you will find some lesson, some message to share with others in a positive light.

Please forgive me for any omissions or errors. Blessings and peace to all who read the words captured herein.

CHAPTER 24

Memories of Mama

Memories of Mama shared from social media, letters, and messages.

Today, I stand on the shoulders of Susie Piper. I am a National Correspondent covering television, film & music because of this young lady. I've also been promoted to Entertainment Editor for one of my outlets.

She asked my daughter and I to write for the St. James Missionary Baptist Church newsletter – The Reflections – many years ago. She gave me my first start, followed by Tommy Wyatt, The Villager & Black Registry Company. I can never forget my beginnings...never. Good night, Sis. Piper. We will see you again. ☺☺ (NR)

All Is Well
"Death is nothing at all,
I have only slipped into the next room
I am I and you are you
Whatever we were to each other, that we are still."
Written by: Henry Scott Holland
I love you, MawMaw. You are loved, remembered and missed. #RIHP (SC)

I'll treasure you always! Enjoy your room in God's palace! 💔 (DM)

Mrs. Piper you'll be missed. But your beautiful spirit will never be forgotten. ♥(PAE)

Life tried to crush her, but only succeeded in creating a diamond.

John Mark Green

Attending the home going services for Ms. Susie Piper (MC)

Tammy, so very sorry to hear of the loss of Mrs. Piper. She made such an impact on so many lives! What blessing she has been you, your family, friends, and her community. Just last week, someone shared the Aycock yearbook on Facebook. As I looked through the pages, I saw the same lady who was my teacher wearing many different hats. She inspired many in her years of teaching and beyond. I know you will miss her. (VK)

I am most grateful that the Lord allowed my family's lives to be positively enriched by Sis. Piper. She will be greatly missed and never forgotten. (PF)

Today, we're saying our earthly farewells to my Austin mother/mentor, Sis. Susie Emma Sansom-Piper. God BLESSED her 98 years to pour into so many of us. Before she left us, she published this book, When A Loved One Dies. Rest in Heaven….until we meet again. (LL)

Mrs. Piper was a curator before we ever understood what that was or how important it was to our history. One of the beautiful things is that her works will live on. (OB)

Today, we paid tribute to a legend. Mrs. Piper, your rich history in Rockdale will never be forgotten. Rest easy Queen. (SM)

Today, we paid tribute to a legend. Mrs. Piper, your rich history in Rockdale will never be forgotten. Rest easy Queen. (SM)

Such a jewel with such wisdom and knowledge…. she shared so many stories.

What an awesome tribute to a wonderful lady and an awesome teacher. She loved teaching and she loved her students unconditional. (DB)

You behaved in that class. She made you want to learn. (RL)

She was my [teacher] at Aycock and at R.J.H. and we was friends and she served as teacher for grades one through twelve and in almost every department of Aycock school to know her is to love her. (RM)

Mrs. Susie Piper was a woman of many chapters in her lifetime, all of wisdom, of history and so much more. True words always she spoke, and so many listen and learned. (BC).

I had the pleasure of being one of her students, she was the best teacher ever and will be missed by many!!! (GC)

She taught us so much that went beyond the classroom. Some teachers you never forget, and she was one of those ♥👩‍🎓♥ (GBM)

If it wasn't for Mrs. Piper, I would have never made it through school. When I fell behind, not just in her class, she adjusted my attention on school. (SM)

Always cheering me on 😢♥♥♥(Brittany, great-granddaughter, and great-great-granddaughters, Kianna and Brianna)

Sorry to hear that Susie Piper passed away Monday. She had a profound impact on my education and my love of history. I know many folks in and from Rockdale who will say the same.

Lee Nichols

February 11, 2017, Rockdale

I went back home to Rockdale today, and was so excited to see this beautiful lady. She is Susie Piper, she is 95 years young, and was my 7th grade Texas history teacher. She is the premier chronicler of African-American life in Milam County, and a major reason I later got a degree in history from the University of Texas at Austin.

Such a sweet angel, full of so much knowledge and beauty, she shared so many stories….. Rest in Love (BCP)

I'm so sad to hear of the passing of my 7th grade history teacher, Miss Susie Piper. She had the most amazing impact on me. I was such a little shit. She loved and taught me so much. Thank you, Mrs. Piper. (MM)

She was an amazing teacher and writer. (AF)

Teachers like that are so important and make a lasting impression. (JH)

She was amazing… one of my favorite teachers. (ST)

Mrs. Piper was a wonderful person inside and out. (MB)

She made Texas history fun. She was a special teacher no doubt. (ML)

I am saddened that this wonderful woman has gained her angel wings. She was without a doubt one of my favorite teachers growing up and she will be missed. I never forget sitting in your history class… (JH)

Another beautiful angel has gained her wings! Susie Piper, we love you, we are thankful for all the ways you have poured into the generations that came behind you and for all the wisdom you shared with us. Thank you for encouraging us, for loving us, for carrying us, and for sending us! (NC)

Lessons From My History by Shari Seifert

Posted on October 31, 2019, by Racial Justice Ministries

As a Christian, I believe that we are all created in the image of God. Racism and white supremacy are heretical and demonic lies as they serve to say that some people are better than other people. The truth is that we are ALL one body in Christ and that body is hurt by white supremacy and racism. We are ALL hurt by these evils.

A big part of my faith journey as a European Descent Lutheran is to root racism and white supremacy out of myself and to do my part to move us towards the Kingdom of God. A few years ago, a friend on a similar journey encouraged me to learn about the history of my hometown regarding race. Below is my reflection on a slice of history from my hometown of Rockdale–a small community in Central Texas. It involves the life and death of my Texas history teacher and serves as a stark example of how racism and white supremacy harm all of us.

END OF ERA

Legendary writer dies at age 98

Funeral services are set Saturday, Nov. 2, for a revered Rockdale native whose evocative depictions of times gone by—both good and bad—warmed and challenged the hearts of generations.

Piper

Susie Sansom Piper died Monday at age 98. Mrs. Piper authored Black History Month series in *The Reporter* for 42 consecutive years.

Her final series, written just months before her 98th birthday, was published Feb. 28.

The author of numerous books of history, poetry and wisdom, her final book, ironically titled "When A Loved One Dies," was published in September.

The previous month *The Reporter* had sent her some photos for yet another publication she was planning.

She was a retired teacher, having taught in both the Aycock and Rockdale schools.

Mrs. Piper received numerous honors throughout her lifetime. In 2015, at age 94, she was featured speaker as the LBJ Library observed the 50th anniversary of President Johnson signing the Voting Rights Act.

FUNERAL—Services are at 10 a.m. Saturday, Nov. 2, in Austin's St. James Missionary Baptist Church, 3417 East Martin Luther King Jr. Blvd.

Viewing prior to the service. A separate viewing will be scheduled from 1 to 3 p.m. Friday, Nov. 1, at a location yet to be determined at presstime.

Following the Nov. 2 service there will be a meal. Burial will be at Oak Lawn Cemetery in Rockdale.

Flowers/acknowledgments: Tamara Hebert Powell, 1712 Zydeco Drive. Round Rock, TX 78664.

A full obituary will be published next week.

Recently, Susie Piper, my middle school Texas history teacher died at the age of 98. She led a remarkable life and was an amazing teacher. She is one of the reasons I learned early on that white supremacy is a lie and I am so thankful for that lesson. I reached out to her a few years ago and to tell her she and Ms. Petty (a black woman who was my most excellent high school biology teacher) were the best teachers I had from Rockdale. I had some exchanges with Ms. Piper and Emzy Jerome Hebert (her son). We gave each other a few books and I got a history lesson that I sure don't remember ever hearing in school.

I learned from Jerome and Ms. Piper that when school integration happened Ms. Piper had been the principal of the Aycock School. The black school that was shut down. I learned that teachers who were black women were required to have master's degrees and teachers who were black men were required to have PhDs in order to teacher at the newly integrated school in Rockdale. Ms. Piper was put in charge of "the hopeless kids" in study hall in the newly integrated school. She said that they were put in "the black room" which had no windows. I suspect that they wanted her to give up and quit – but that was not in her nature. She told me "It was always my philosophy that everyone counted, and everyone could learn." Somewhere along the way people wised up and put her in the classroom where I benefitted from her excellence in teaching and I am grateful for that. She was a prolific writer and noted historian. She was the keynote speaker at the Lyndon Baines Johnson presidential library on the 50th anniversary of the voting rights act. I am so mad and sad about the injustices she went through. I don't even have the words for this. Mourn maybe the loss of the gifts and treasures we don't have because other Susie Pipers were put in charge of study hall rather than the classroom. I'm angry about her and others' mistreatments. Denying people's gifts and not giving them a chance to shine really hurts all of us. I don't know what happened to move Ms. Piper from study hall to the classroom. I would like to hear that story too. I suspect it took some honest accounting of the situation and some bravery. Let's have more of that please.

Shari is a European descent Lutheran living in Minneapolis with her wife and two sons. She sells houses and dismantles white supremacy in the Lutheran Church. She is on the board of the European Descent Lutheran Association for Racial Justice and the Minneapolis Synod anti-racism table.

Note: Shari Seifert is the author of <u>Ashes to Action: Finding Myself at the Intersection of the Minneapolis Uprising</u>

Last Monday Susie Piper, my middle school Texas History teacher died at the age of 98. She led a remarkable life and was an amazing teacher and she is one of reasons I learned early on that white supremacy is a lie - I am so thankful for that lesson. I reached out to her a few years ago and let her know that I considered she and Ms. Petty (a black woman who was my most excellent high school biology teacher) the best teachers I had from Rockdale. I had some exchanges with Ms. Piper and Emzy Jerome Hebert (her son)- we gave each other some books and I got a history lesson that I sure don't remember ever hearing in school. I learned from Jerome and Ms. Piper that when school integration happened Ms. Piper had been the principal of Aycock School - the black school and this school was shut down. I learned that teachers who were black women were required to have masters degrees and teachers who were black men were required to have PhDs in order to teacher at the newly integrated school in Rockdale. Ms. Piper was put in charge of "the hopeless kids" in study hall in the newly integrated school. She said that they were put in "the black room" which had no windows. I suspect that they wanted her to give up and quit - but that was not in her nature. She told me "It was always my philosophy that everyone counted, and everyone could learn." Somewhere along the way people wised up and put her in the classroom where I benefitted from her excellence in teaching, and I am grateful for that. She was a prolific writer and noted historian. She was the keynote speaker at the LBJ presidential library on 50th anniversary of the voting rights act. I am so mad and sad about the injustice that she went through. I -don't even have the word for this - mourn maybe - the loss of the gifts and treasures we don't have because other Susie Pipers were put in charge of study hall rather than the classroom. I'm angry about her and others' mistreatments. Denying people's gifts and not giving them a chance to shine really hurts all of us. I don't know what happened to move Ms. Piper from study hall to the classroom - I would like to hear that story too - I suspect it took some honest accounting of the situation and some bravery. Let's have more of that please. (KEC)

My heart is heavy with grief and joy at the same time! I grieve with my friend, Tamara Hebert Powell and with all of us who were blessed to have had her beloved grandmother and brother in our lives! I have joy knowing that Ms. Piper and Jerome are once again together, with their other loved ones! Ms. Susie Piper was so much more than an educator, she was love and wisdom! We kept in touch, and it always meant so much to me when I received a letter or card from her! She spoke of "all of her children!" Consider yourself very BLESSED if you ever found yourself in the company of this magnificent lady! I will miss her on so many levels! The last words she said to me as I was leaving after our visit were, "You'll always have a place to stay." I'll forever cherish and treasure Ms. Susie Piper! Your love, kindness, and knowledge will be with me for eternity! (DM)

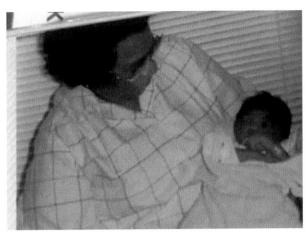  

Many of y'all may know how it feels to grow up with your grandmother. But I got the honor to grow up with my great grandmother. We did everything together! She taught me how to read, write (my cursive), math and draw. She took me to piano classes every Saturday from age 5 to 12 years old. She even took me to singing lessons.

My mama would come to my school and talk about black history... my mama was the BEST teacher. She taught for 44 years so I knew I had the best teacher. She made my clothes in elementary, she never ever went a year without sending me a birthday card, valentine or Christmas card OR gift.... Even at age 33 she would write me and the girls checking on us. My mama taught me how to draw because she knew how to draw the best art work! She made the best spaghetti, and pancakes and hamburgers. We had fun going to vacation bible school and church choir practice...My mama would take me with her everywhere, I guess you can say I had the best summers because my mama was a celebrity in my eyes! Which of course made me a celebrity too... everyone in town loved my Mama... she taught moms, dads uncles, nieces nephews, sisters and brothers and their kids. Everyone loved my mama but she was my Mama and I was her ONLY great grandchild. She would tell everyone about when I was a baby I would call HEB...b*tchy B 😊 or how I called McDonalds... Popeyes Donald. She never missed a game or concert I had even in college. She helped me move into Southern University my freshman year. My mama was there for both births of her great great granddaughters. She not only helped with raising me... she helped with raising Ki and Bri aka Legs and Dancing Doll ♥. I love my mama sooooo much. We could talk for hours, me her and uncle Romey. 😊😊😊 Like I said it was a honor I had the best loving, caring genuine, positive, humble, giving, sweetest, confident, strong 98 year old GREAT grandmother ever!

Notable Rockdalians from Aycock High School

My students were many both at the Rockdale Junior High and Aycock High. Their accomplishments abound. Many of the Aycock students were featured in the years of Black History writings in the Rockdale Reporter from Ebony Etchings to the Other Side of the Tracks. Former students of Aycock left an indelible print on the sands of time. Their services on the other side of the tracks will always remain as a reminder of things left behind. Although their contributions may not be engraved in stone, they will somehow be woven into future generations. During this period, this group brought a sense of pride to their community, for they proved that where there was a will, there is also a way. Love and cooperation still existed during these years. These are but a few that I can name, but many more have notable contributions to the states and abroad.

NOTE: This is transcribed from the handwriting and typings of Susie E. Sansom Piper. There are many notable Aycock ex-students and this is only a sample of the many accomplishments attained by those who matriculated there.

Eural Norman Davis, Harry Wayne Jones, Johnny Lee, and Blanche Tally were gold medal winners at the State Interscholastic League Activities at Prairie View A&M University. They became well-known for their singing talent. Davis was the first Black to participate in the Drake relays. Aycock graduate Eural Davis (class of 1940) was known as the 'Jackie Robinson of track.' In 1947—the year Robinson integrated baseball— Davis became the first African-American to travel with an integrated track team. He was sixth in the Olympic long jump trials the next year. He went on to a long career teaching and coaching and is a member of the Prairie View A&M and Rockdale Athletic Halls of Honor. He was inducted into the Prairie View A&M Sports Hall of fame in 1989.

Ralphell Johnson, was hired as coach and teacher of Social Studies, Health, and Biology in 1951 at Aycock. He was the only male coach at Aycock from 1951 through 1956. He coached football, basketball, baseball, softball, track, and field. During the five year period, many records were set. Many of the athletes under his leadership became a "first" in history from the Rockdale area and in the professional athletic programs of the nation. During the 1955-56 football season, his team defeated Snooks High School of urleson County, with a score of 156-0, thus setting an unheard of state and national record in football scores.

James Leroy Wright was recruited by many colleges for basketball and football. He went to the University of the Pacific (formerly known as College of the Pacific). He led the nation in rebounding during his junior and senior years and as of 2006 his rebounding record had not been broken. He was drafted in the 3rd round to play basketball with the Boston Celtics, even after a knee injury. He also played basketball with New York, Philadelphia, and Indiana, and served as assistant coach for the Minneapolis Pipers. He was inducted into the University of Pacific Hall of Fame in 1988.

Frank Charles McKee accepted a scholarship to play football for Prairie View A&M College. He made all Southwest Conference Team for one year, and All American for two years. He was drafted by the Dallas Texans (Kansas City Chiefs) and played for one year.

Billy Ray Locklin played football for New Mexico State University. He was one of their most outstanding athletes, and was also inducted into their Hall of Fame. He was drafted to play for the Oakland Raiders. He later went on to Canada and played for four years with the Montreal Alouenes. He also spent two years with the NFL Denver Broncos.

Ora Viola Scott, a teacher and reading specialist, was among the first Blacks to become a part of the Texas Education Agency during their early integration of schools.

Jew Don Boney, City Councilman Houston; James E. Johnson, College Professor, Houston; Hubert Glenn Lovelady, Chemist and Inventor; Lillian Bacy, Registered Nurse, Houston; Florida

Lonnie Johnson, Artist/Sculptor, California

Other students included Emily Banks, Allie Banks Powell, Bertha Thomas Klein, Eula Sansom Hebert,all registered nurses. Helen M. Crayton Rhem, Johnny Black I; Pearly M. Hines ; Mildred Wilhite Lovelady; Matthew Cook; Samuel Tucker; Fanny Lovelady Spain, Margaret Sanders Green, Sharon Williams-Stein, Barbara Sansom Holsome, and Oscar E. Wilhight all educators in Texas, Arizona, Mississippi, and California. Lynn Scott, Pharmacist, Abilene. City Councilman Leo Gadsen served a lifetime in the Armed Services, Clifford Norwood, US Air Force.

Athletics included William Preston Moultrie, Coach for Howard University and Stanford University; Billy Jean Walton, Billy Ray Locklin, Frank C. McKee, and James Lee Wright were professional football and basketball players.

Bob Robertson, Elma Lee Moultrie-Postal Supervisors, Arizona and Texas; Lucy Ray Crawford and Billy Eugene Gray, business owners in California and Texas; John F. Williams, Engineer.

George Lee Molden, Lawrence Bacy, Overton Smith and David Smith, Ministers in South Carolina, Oklahoma, and California.

Marie E. Moore, Texas Highway Department; James Lee Molden and Lovie Molden-Edwards Law Officials in Texas.

Betty Louise Smith Williams was Rockdale's first black female city council member.

Wherever they chose to live, they still created a historical impact on their hometown. Many more have followed to make a notable and tremendous impact on the world since the days of integration. Lawyers, Artists, Musicians, Doctors, Nurses, Executives, and many more hail from the legacy of their Rockdale ancestors. This small Milam County community has produced a legacy of excellence and accomplishment for which all can be proud.

Historical Information:

Tributes were set up in Rockdale in honor of these citizens:

- Julius Moultry Park – Baxter Street behind the old Aycock High School
- Sumuel Park- MLK and Fifth Street, contributed by ancestors of the late Jack Shields
- Blacksmith Trip Hammer- In Memory of Julius Moultry, Rockdale Museum
- Old IG&N depot is now Rockdale Historical Museum

Paul Moultry

Julius "Bose" Moultry

Julius "Bose" Moultry, WWI

Eula Bell Crayton Moultry

Eula Bell Crayton Moultry

Eula Bell Crayton Moultry

Susie and Eula

Photo-Eula Ammie Sansom Hebert

**The Sansoms E.J., Susie, Barbara Sue,
and Eula Ammie**

Ready for the band show Barbara and Eula

**Eula and Barbara graduate
from High School**

Susie Moultry Sansom Circa 1941

Eula Ammie Sansom Hebert

Eula Ammie, ready for the dance

Susie Emma Moultry
Sansom

Susie Emma Sansom

Cousin, Pee Wee Crayton

Emzy James Sansom

Aycock Classroom

Practice makes perfect, blackboard drills

Aycock Recess

Aycock Students

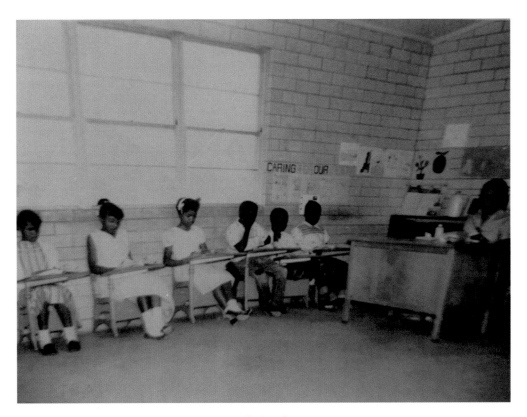

Aycock Students

Old Rockdale Jr. High

Aycock Float

Aycock Homecoming

Old Aycock High School

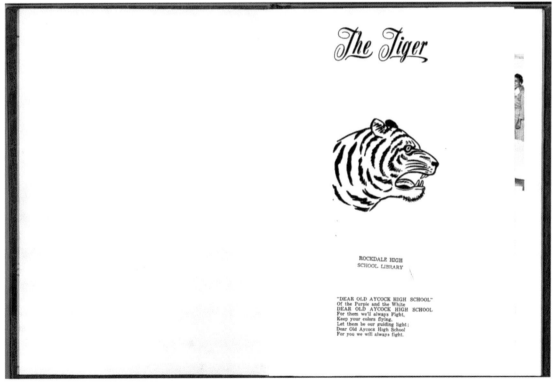

Top photos are Aycock's only yearbook

Top photos are Aycock's only yearbook

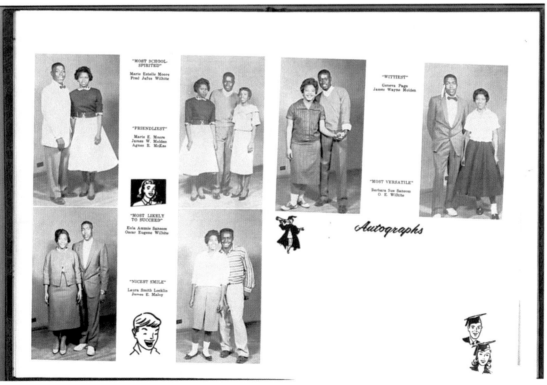

Top photos are Aycock's only yearbook

Top photos are Aycock's only yearbook

Barbara Holsome, daughter, Mama, grandchildren (Tamara, Cynthia, Jerome Welton Jr., and Anthony and great grandchild, Brittany, and great great grands Kianna and Brianna)

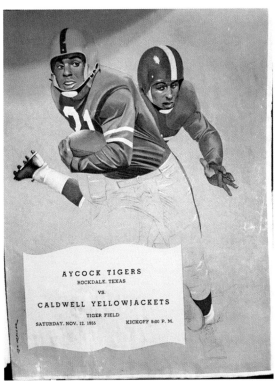

Aycock 1955 Football Program

Julius Moultry's Blacksmith Shop and Paul Moultry's Arvil – Institute of Texan Culture

Light Bread Hat

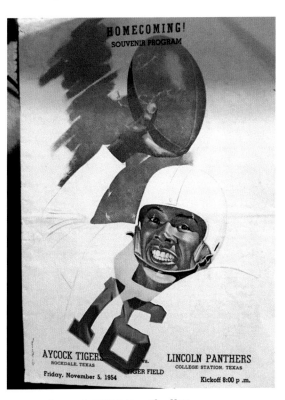

Aycock 1955 Football Program

Tamara and Jerome

**Rev. John Piper, Susie, and
church members at church anniversary**

**Mama Susie, pa-pa Emzy James, and three
gradnchildren- Tamara, Jerome, and Cynthia**

Craft savvy always seeing beautiful things

Susie Sansom Piper - Age 97

Cynthia, Tamara, and Mama

Mama Susie, Jeroma, Tamara

great great grands Kianna and Brianna

Jerome, Mama, and Beauty

**Mama with her heart, Brittany Eula Norris,
Her only Great granddaughter, and great
great granddaughters, Kianna and Brianna**

Mama Susie and Jerome

Susie Sansom Piper, Luci Baines Johnson and Emzy Jerome Hebert

90th birthday, Mama and Aycock students

**August 2019 African American
History Museum Washington DC**

Age 97

Playing piano for church

Speaking engagements

50th Anniversary of Voter's Rights Act LBJ library Susie Sansom Piper and Luci Baines Johnson

**Speaking at LBJ Library,
Austin Texas**

Directing Choir Circa 2017

Paul Moultry Signage Moultry Park, Rockdale, Texas

Horse drawn Carriage and Pall Bearers

Final Funeral Procession, horse drawn carriage Susie Sansom Piper is laid to rest

When a Loved one Dies" grief book

Casket and Vault

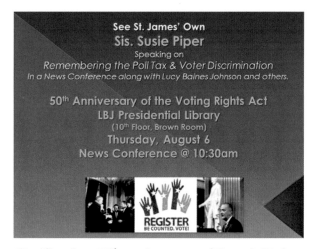

Notification 50th anniversary of Voter's Rights Speaking Engagement

Funeral Program

Susie – Sansom – Piper Day Proclamation

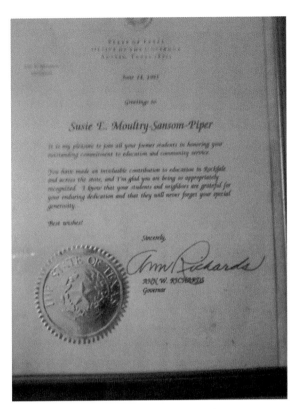

Certificate of Recognition from the Governor

Outstanding Teacher of Texas History

Student Government Award

Certificate of Citation from the House of Representatives for nursing work

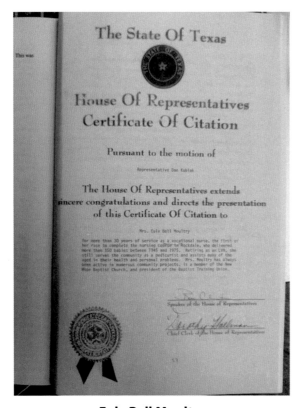

Eula Bell Moultry

Susie Sansom Piper

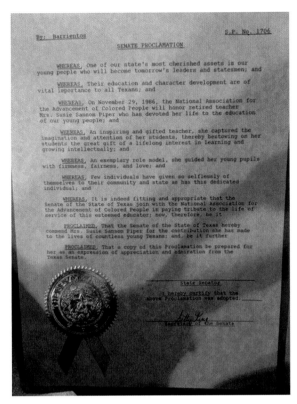

Senate Proclamation – to Honor Susie

**Marriage License of Julius Moultry
and Eula Belle Crayton**

My Dear Mr. Santa Caus: I am writing you to tell you what I want for Christmas. I have some very nice teachers. Their names are Mrs. E. D. Siedel, Mrs. C. M. Allen and Mrs. E. M. B. Mays. Please don't forget to bring them something nice for Christmas. I am 11 years old and am in the 7th grade. I want some shoes, stockings, a doll and some fireworks. I want a coat and hat, some gloves and I want a sweater, too. And Santa, I have a mother and a father. Please don't forget to bring my aunties, grandmothers and grandfather and uncles. Santa, I hope I am not asking for too much. Bring Opal some gloves. Yours truly, Susie Emma Moultry, Rockdale, Texas.

Future Writer, Young Susie's letter to Santa

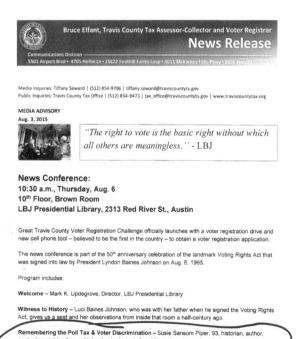

**Remembering the Poll Tax & Voter
Discrimination – Susie Sansom Piper**

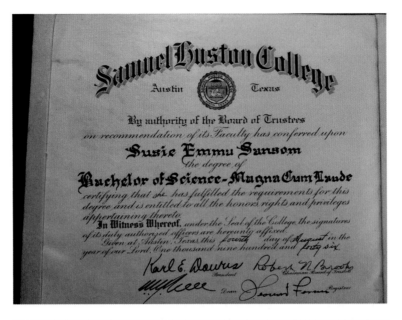

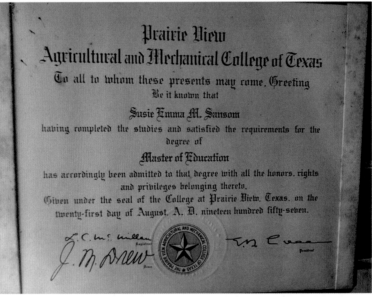

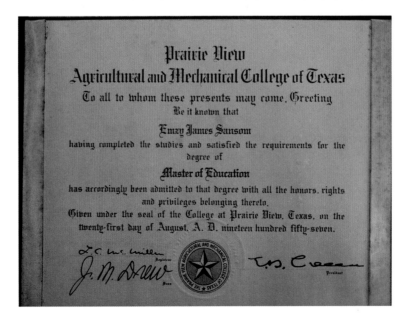

Obituary for EMZY JAMES SANSOM (Aged 56)

EMZY JAMES SANSOM

ROCKDALE—Funeral for Emzy James Sansom, 56, will be Saturday at 2 p.m. in Murray Street Church of Christ with Minister Thomas Wright officiating. Burial in Oaklawn cemetery.

He died Monday in Tomball.

He has been a teacher in Milam County schools for 29 years.

Survivors include his widow; three daughters, Mrs. Barbara Sue Holsome, Omaha, Neb., Mrs. Eula Annie Hebert, Rockdale, and Mrs. Flosetta McDaniel, Odessa; two brothers, Don Sansom, Fort Worth, and Claude T. Sansom, San Francisco, Calif.; six sisters, Mrs. Lone Venable, Temple, Okla., Mrs. Willie Marshal, Temple, Mrs. Celester Perry, Temple, Mrs. Arilene Nixon, Crockett, Miss Hattie Sansom, Fort Worth, and Mrs. Rubie Banks, Rockdale; and 13 grandchildren.

Segregation signs

JIM CROW LAWS

"IT SHALL BE UNLAWFUL for a negro and white person to play together or in company with each other in any game of cards or dice, dominoes or checkers."

BIRMINGHAM, ALABAMA, 1930

"IT SHALL BE UNLAWFUL for any white prisoner to be handcuffed or otherwise chained or tied to a negro prisoner."

ARKANSAS, 1903

"NO COLORED BARBER shall serve as a barber to white women or girls."

ATLANTA, GEORGIA, 1926

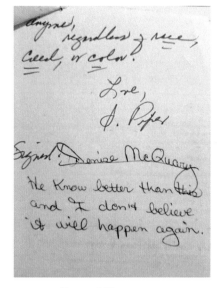

Parent Response

Write it over until you get it

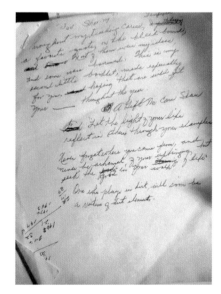

Saga of a Black Woman

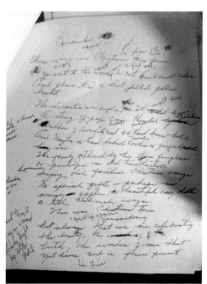

Susie's thoughts

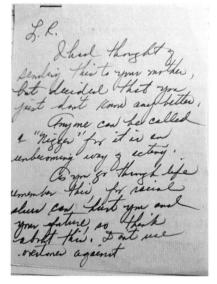

Susie's thoughts

**Mrs. Piper's note to student
Vs. Student note**

Susie Sansom-Piper

August 23, 1921- October 21,2019

Was a lifelong educator and consummate professional. Mrs. Sansom-Piper attended Aycock High School and graduated in 1937 as a salutatorian of her class. She received an Associate's Degree in Business Administration, graduating with honors, from St. Phillips Junior College, San Antonio, Texas in 1940. In 1946, she graduated Magna Cum Laude from Samuel Huston College (now Huston-Tillotson University), Austin, Texas, receiving a Bachelors of Science Degree in Business Administration.

A Master's Degree was conferred with honors from Prairie View A&M College in Administration and Elementary Education in 1956 along with a Counselor Certification and additional studies under the National Science Foundation Program in Science and Mathematics. Mrs. Sansom-Piper's teaching career began and extended entirely in the Rockdale Public School System. For 42 years, Susie taught in the Rockdale, Texas Public School System. As a historian, she chronicled the lives and accomplishments of African American students in the local newspaper for 41 years. She started in 1943 at Aycock High School, when a replacement teacher was needed for grades three through five and music. For 23 years, she served in various capacities teaching grades three through eight; high school, science, social studies, business education, and music. She also assisted in the educational testing program and served as bookkeeper-secretary for many years. Through her teaching, manifested by patience and kindness, many students were district and state winners in University Interscholastic League events.

A prolific writer, she featured such writings as Way Back When, Ebony Etchings, Just Folks, From Valleys to Mountains, and numerous articles. Her writings included 41 years of newspaper features in the Rockdale Reporter, writing and editing church bulletins, and newsletters. She was passionate and worked tirelessly to educate others about the great contributions our people have made to society, and to know of the great and noteworthy Milam County citizens.

This work is a compilation of the auto-biography she began over 50 years ago, transcription of her story, and culmination of her life's work to educate others. Prior to her death, at the age of 98, she published When a Loved One Dies, with her grand-daughter Tamara and began the last phase of her legacy work Seventeen Years in the Black Room.

Mrs. Piper won numerous awards, certificates, and honors for her work over the many decades.

Tamara S. Powell

Tamara Powell is a native of Rockdale Texas. She is the grand-daughter of noted historian, Susie Sansom-Piper. Tamara spent her formative years in the Rockdale Independent School District winning numerous awards in Science and Academics.

She was the first African American editor of the Rockdale Yearbook, as well as, the first winner of the Regional Science Fairs for Rockdale during her school years. Graduating with honors.

She attended the University of Texas on a Texas Achievement Award Scholarship, and Huston Tillotson College for the Welch Science Foundation, graduating with a Bachelor of Science Degree in English and Chemistry with specific course work in Organizational Communication. She also holds a Master's of Science Degree in Oriental Medicine and herbology.

Tamara later went on to a promising executive level career in the private sector and government where she has utilized her speaking, writing, and problem- solving skills to implement new initiatives and deliver high profile projects. She also owns an Acupuncture Clinic (Acufit- Capital City Wellness) in the Austin Area.

Tamara is an avid reader and writer. Her latest projects include When a Loved One Dies, (Principles for Steering through Grief (available from Tamara or on Amazon.com and BN.com) and completing the memoires of her grandmother, Seventeen Years in the Black Room (Bridging the gap from Integration).

Tamara is the mother of one daughter, Brittany, and three grand-daughters, Kianna,Brianna, and Sierra. She currently resides in Round Rock, Tx.

Printed in the United States
by Baker & Taylor Publisher Services